Promises to Keep

Developing the Skills of Marriage

Kathleen R. Fischer and Thomas N. Hart

Jim and Pat,
Blessings on the
journey. We believe in
marriage. We believe
in you.

Love,
Tom & Kathy

Paulist Press
New York/Mahwah

Library of Congress Cataloging-in-Publication Data

Fischer, Kathleen R., 1940–
    Promises to keep : developing the skills of marriage / Kathleen R. Fischer and Thomas N. Hart.
       p.   cm.
    Includes bibliographical references.
    ISBN 0-8091-3288-5
    1. Married people—Religious life. 2. Marriage—Religious aspects—Christianity. 3. Intimacy—Religious aspects—Christianity. 4. Marriage (Psychology)
    5. Intimacy (Psychology) I. Hart, Thomas N. II. Title.
BV4596.M3F57   1991
248.8'44—dc20   91-27075
                                           CIP

Published by Paulist Press
997 Macarthur Boulevard
Mahwah, NJ 07430

Printed and bound in the
United States of America

Contents

Introduction

From the time we are fairly young, many of us dream of meeting a wonderful person someday, falling in love, marrying and having a family, and living happily ever after. It is a dream of hearing those magic words, "I love you," and of being close, warm, supported, companioned, and cherished for the rest of our days.

Most of us do meet someone and do hear the magic words. Filled with warm feelings and with hope, we gather our friends and in their presence we make a promise. It is what unfolds from there that we have our difficulties with, for it does not always correspond with the rest of our dream. How far it often diverges is shown in the fact that about half of marriages in the west today end in divorce. How is that to be explained?

Successful marriage depends on three crucial things: 1) your choice of partner, 2) the attitudes you bring, and 3) the skills you develop. Most of you who pick up this book have already chosen your mate, so what we concentrate on here are the attitudes and skills you will need. But let us look briefly at all three of the crucial factors.

The partner you choose must be someone who is basically compatible with you. That means someone who shares most of your values and at least some of your interests, who wants roughly the same things out of life that you do, and whose personality and style are ones you feel comfortable with in most situations. It usually takes a year or two of being together in a variety of circumstances to discover whether that compatibility is there or not. To make the assessment, you have to know yourself fairly well and have some judgment about others. If you twinge a bit reading over this description because your

1

choice is made and it was not perfect, it might be some consolation to know that no one else is enjoying a perfect match either.

The attitudes you bring to marriage are just as crucial in determining success or failure. Life is challenging, and it does not cease to be so when two lives are joined and more lives are generated. If the increased complexity adds to your joys, it also adds to your trials. If you are going to keep your promises, you will need courage, hope, and perseverance. Living with another requires generosity, forgiveness, and patience. Reasonable expectations are a great help, too. All of these are spiritual attitudes, virtues, habits of the mind and heart. They are the measure of the quality of the person. You do not need to be religious to possess or to be earnest about fostering them, but because they do not come easily, religion can be a vital stimulus and support.

Marital success depends also upon certain skills. You need skill in communicating, in negotiating differences, in problem-solving. You need skill in raising children, balancing work and family, dealing with in-laws and friends. You need skill in working on your own growth as a person. As with the attitudes, you already have some measure of these skills when you marry, but you have to develop them further if you want to succeed.

The aim of this book is to help you cultivate the attitudes and skills needed for a happy marriage. In it we draw on our own married experience and that of the countless couples we have worked with in counseling and marriage enrichment events over many years. We incorporate what we consider the best insights of religious and psychological writers on marriage. It is our conviction that these are mutually enriching sources for understanding and living out our marriage promises, since what God wants for our relationships is what we also want—that they be happy and growthful.

You may pick up this book with the sense that your marriage is not all that it could be, that there are still significant parts of your dream which you have not realized. You may be quite satisfied with your relationship in general, but aware of a few trouble spots you must deal with. You might be in crisis, and feel the need for help in navigating unfamiliar waters. Or you might simply want something to read that will get you and your mate thinking and talking about all the important aspects of your relationship so that you can revitalize and deepen it. This book is designed to speak to all of these concerns.

It is a book at once spiritual and practical, the practicalities in the forefront, the spirituality in the background. In the first chapter, we spell out the sort of integrated spirituality we envision. After that we get down to practical matters, with the spirituality continuing to constitute the context. Each chapter is brief and ends with an exercise for you to do as a couple. We suggest you read a chapter a week together, do the exercise, and discuss your relationship with regard to the chapter's themes. You can rejoice in your successes and pinpoint areas of growth you would like to work on together.

We would like to thank all the couples whose experiences have contributed to the insights of this book. Their lives are a primary resource for developing a down-to-earth spirituality of marriage, and their struggles and breakthroughs can enrich couples everywhere. In telling their stories we have changed their names and other identifying information to assure confidentiality.

The poet Rainer Maria Rilke once remarked that the attempt of one human being to love another is perhaps the most difficult of tasks—but the work for which everything else is but preparation. Jesus tells us throughout the gospels that the deepest purpose of our lives is to learn how to love others well. When we do that, we not only come to know and cherish one another, but come to know and love God as well. This learning to love another human being well is the adventure of marriage. We hope our suggestions will improve the quality of that adventure for you.

Chapter 1
Living a Married Spirituality

$$\diamond$$

There are two aspects of marriage we particularly emphasize in this book. The first is the skills on which marital success depends, and in that we will try to be as practical and helpful as possible. The second is the spiritual dimension of marriage, and in that we will try to be as integrated as possible, that is, we will try to show how the spiritual dimension is not something superadded to a marriage, but rather something already embedded in the day-to-day lived experience, a reality to be recognized and responded to.

We do not focus very much on prayer, churchgoing, faith-sharing, or good works couples may do for others. We see great value in all these activities, knowing how helpful they can be in fostering a vital and lasting marriage. But this is already clear, and would be accepted by most Christian couples. In fact, it is what many understand by "marital spirituality."

We are calling attention to something that is less obvious, that is, in fact, overlooked by many who want to live a spiritual life. Less obvious though it is, it is more pervasive, and has as much or more significance for our life with God. That is the spiritual dimension that is already intrinsic to married life as lived on a daily basis, whether it is adverted to or not. It is something already deep within

5

both the lovemaking and the arguments, within the chaotic household and the exasperating workplace, within the struggle to understand and accept one another and the quiet joy we often feel in each other's company, within the fatigue we experience getting up in the night to attend to the crying infant and the warmth we feel when our mate does something thoughtful, within the endless scraping it takes to meet the bills and the best moments of family gatherings. We are referring to how God is present and active in all of that whether we realize it or not. Our hope is that all of us might become more aware of that, so that we can recognize the sacredness of the ordinary and more fully correspond with it.

But catching this vision of things may demand making some significant shifts in the way we have usually mapped spiritual reality. Let us look at that more closely.

A Theology of Marriage

First, God is not up in the skies or out in space somewhere, but right here where we are. God is within the system of things in which we live, for that is where God has always been experienced. "God is not far from any of us, for in God we live, and move, and have our being" (Acts 17:27–28). In spite of all this religious experience and this statement from a sermon of St. Paul, we may still slip into viewing the relationship between God and the world as that between "the monarch and his realm." Then we have to bring ourselves back to recognizing that God is much closer to us than that, that God is the mystery immersed in the depths of all reality. God is the source of creativity, the font of all energy, in this material realm in which we live. God is present to the world much more the way the soul is present in the body than the way the monarch is present to his realm. So if I am looking for

God, a good place to look is within me. And if I want to
hear the voice of God, I am more likely to hear it coming
to me from within my own being than from the skies.

Correspondingly, God does not intervene occasionally in our affairs, as, for example, in answer to prayer, the
rest of the time just letting the machinery of the world
run. God is present and active always and everywhere,
wanting what is good for us and working to bring it
about. God's dedication to our cause, and the human
cause generally, is neither something we have to wring by
cajoling nor earn by a blameless life. It is given because
God wishes to give it, and is always there to be recognized and accepted. Thus, the God human beings have
come to know through the generations is neither indiffer-
ent, nor harsh and judgmental, but gracious and kind and
actively working for our good.

And so, it is more accurate to think of God, not as
having created the world, but as creating it all the time.
For if you ask what God is doing in the depths of all
reality, the answer is that God is toiling to make something beautiful. Did God create Yellowstone National
Park? No, God is still creating it. It is much different
today than it was a thousand years ago. And you will not
find it the same next year as you found it last year. God
has already been working on Yellowstone for two-and-a-
half billion years—there is some stone in the park which
is that old. Yellowstone has gone through countless trans-
formations and developments in that time. And the creative work continues.

It is the same with God's quiet activity in the depths
of human life. We probably see it most readily in the
development of the embryo through all the stages of preg-
nancy, a wonder to our eyes. But it goes on no less mar-
velously through all the stages of an infant's growth into

a child, and a child's growth through adolescence into adulthood. Then is it over? We hope not! For God's main interest where a human being is concerned is not the growth of the body but of the person within, and that growth is open-ended all through a person's life (and possibly through the next life, too). In synergy with God, we are always creating ourselves, as we interact with the circumstances of our lives.

Our circumstances may be marriage. If so, we are living our life in close relationship with one other human being, and possibly also with children. This is one of the situations in which we experience God's creative action and have a choice about whether we want to give ourselves to it or not. In marriage two individuals grapple with each other as well as with their environment, and in the interaction are consciously or unconsciously instruments to each other of God's creative activity. In what we might call the "crucible of intimacy," because it is often hot and changes us from what we were, we affirm, challenge, support, frustrate, assist, break, block, and stretch each other, all within the ambience of God's sustaining and creative love. Neither of us can remain the same in all this spirited exchange, even from one year to the next. It is nothing less than the winds, rains, upheavals, geysers, runoff, fires, snows, and earthquakes of Yellowstone. The outcome God hopes and toils for with us in all this is human potential fully actualized—better persons, better lovers—and the crucible is part of the process.

Human growth and spiritual growth are one. Spirituality is not something optional which may be added to our humanity; it is an essential component of our humanity, and it is expressed *within* a fully realized humanity. Wherever you find a beautiful human person, you are immediately aware of spiritual components in that person's makeup. You see love, hope, generosity, humility, faithfulness, serenity, honesty, steadfastness, self-transcendence. Where you see these qualities, you know you have a truly spiritual person. But without these qualities would you have a fully *human* person? No. Full humanity and rich spirituality are one and the same. In discussing spirituality, we are not talking about the frosting, but about the cake itself. We are talking about human possibility fully realized.

Marriage as Sacrament

In the Roman Catholic tradition, marriage is a sacrament. Here is what that means. Any sacrament is some visible embodiment of the presence and power of God. The waters of baptism, for example, are the visible embodiment of God's action of purifying a person desiring to be a Christian, as well as of God's taking that person symbolically through the experience of dying and rising again, to signify entrance into the Christian community and a complete change of life. The bread and wine of the eucharist are the visible embodiments of the body and blood of Christ given to us as nourishment.

What is the visible embodiment or sacrament in marriage? There is no bread, wine, water, nor oil here. The visible embodiments of God in marriage are nothing other than the two persons who are giving themselves to one another. They are the sacred thing. Each embodies the presence and action of God for the other, and so what they give each other is holy. This may sound strange, for we are all sinful and scarcely feel holy. Yet we are made in the image of God, and as Christians are children of God and members of the body of Christ. Something of God is expressed in us. That is the basis of the sacramentality of marriage. When we are deeply loved by someone, the love of God for us becomes tangible in a human love, and the creative action of God on us begins to appear in very significant measure through that person. The same thing has happened to that person by reason of our love for them.

So if the meaning of marriage is that we are to embody as a sacrament the love that God has for our mate, how do we do it? Who will show us how? The person who did it best is Jesus of Nazareth. To all who came to know him, he was a powerful sacrament of God's presence and love. How? He was accepting of people as they were, forgiving, faithful in friendship. He was gentle and nurturing, yet honestly confrontational at times. He was patient. He was generous, sharing all he had. Thus, even though he was not married, he shows us a beautiful ideal of married love. The gospels give us many memorable images of how Jesus expressed his love for individuals and groups. He was sacrament par excellence. We are sacrament. For God is not out there but in here, in the depths of all reality, seeking self-expression particularly in human beings.

What is said here is conveyed in specifically Christian terms. But what is at the heart of it will sound somehow already familiar to persons everywhere who recognize a transcendent reality at the source of their lives and strive to correspond with it; who sense a gracious mystery at the core of all things and know moments of unmistakable encounter with the holy, who are familiar with the lives of some of the great men and women of the world's religious traditions who have been especially aware of, conformed to, and expressive of the transcendent.

In summary, when we talk about the spiritual in this book, we are not talking mainly about religious activities as a special area of life. We are talking about the stuff of everyday life at the level of its deepest significance. Our hope is that all of us, by becoming more aware of it, might also be more responsive to it, so that the gracious purposes of God might be realized in us.

The contrast between these two different spiritual emphases is brought out nicely in a story from Sufi mysticism. There was a man whose love for truth was so great that he traveled far and wide to be able to talk to scholars of the Koran and learn all he could from them. He would come home and earnestly accost people in the marketplace to discuss the truths of his faith. One day his wife told him how unfairly he was treating her—only to learn that her husband had no interest whatsoever in that kind of truth.

EXERCISE 1: FINDING GOD IN YOUR MARRIAGE

In the Acts of the Apostles we are told that "God is not far from any of us, for in God we live and move and have our being" (17:27–28). Use this verse for some moments of prayerful reflection on your own marriage, and see if you can name the spiritual gifts and challenges found in it. Then share the results of your reflection with your partner.

The following questions may help:
1. How does the love of your spouse make God's love visible and tangible for you?
2. When, in your marriage, have you felt yourself called to conversion or forgiveness?

3. What are the ways in which your marriage gives you hope and courage?

4. How have you and your spouse experienced the paschal mystery of Christ, i.e., the process of death/resurrection, in your marital relationship?

Chapter 2

Growing in Intimacy

───────── ◇ ─────────

One of our deepest human longings is for closeness to someone. It is the opposite of loneliness, which is perhaps our greatest suffering. Loneliness is the feeling that I am all alone, that I am cut off and cannot get connected, that nobody cares about me. Intimacy is the feeling that I am closely tied to at least one person, that life is something we share, that what happens to me matters very much to this person and vice versa.

Much of the power of sex over us is the promise it holds of the intimacy we long for. Sex means the other person is naked to me, without protective cover, totally available. Sex means full freedom to see and to be seen, to touch and to be touched, to be so close as to have full body contact, indeed to be in some measure inside one another. This is an immense comfort. Sex is a wonderful *symbol* of intimacy. But, as we know, symbols can be empty of real meaning.

For what we *really* want is to enjoy this kind of togetherness at an emotional/spiritual level. We can have sex with someone we hardly know, and it feels very good physically yet leaves us still lonely when it is over. By contrast, we can share our very souls with someone else and end by feeling wonderfully close and cared for, though there has been no physical contact at all. This reaches a deeper level of need and its satisfaction abides longer. Sex has a powerful hold on our psyches precisely because it suggests and symbolizes all this, speaking unconsciously to our profound longing. When sex *goes with* a real heart-to-heart communing of persons, as the bodily expression and celebration of that more inward sharing of life, it is at its most exciting and satisfying.

A salesman who had never been married but had had many sexual partners in his travels, mentioned in counseling that he was not having sex with these women anymore. That decision was the outgrowth of a whole process of personal development. He was overcoming his low self-esteem and beginning to like and value himself more. Correspondingly, he was developing more reverence for others. Meanwhile, a genuine non-sexual friendship started growing between him and a woman who had been an acquaintance for years. Though he was still alone on the road a lot, he couldn't have casual sex anymore. It now seemed empty, meaningless, and harmful to his spirit as well as that of his casual partner. This was a remarkable change in him, a rising to a higher level of humanness.

Intimacy: What Makes It So Difficult?

The heart-to-heart sharing that constitutes genuine interpersonal intimacy does not come easily to most of us. It frightens us on several scores, and we shy away.

1. When I open my heart, I make myself vulnerable. What I say can be misunderstood, used against me, or lightly dismissed. It can be found ridiculous, bad, or boring. And once it's out, it's out; I cannot call it back and restore it to its hiding place. So sharing myself is a risk; it takes courage. Obviously, I need to be careful whom I do this with. I must have reasonable assurance that I am safe, that this is someone I can trust.

But, of course, intimacy is mutual. My partner needs exactly the same kind of loving receiver. I myself need to be interested, reverent, nonjudgmental, and trustworthy—hard things. I cannot ever use against the person what is ventured in trust. When we receive another in this way, we embody God's own unconditional interest and acceptance.

2. If I get too close, I will be swallowed up. I will lose myself, being taken over by you. I will no longer know who I am. I will no longer have a life of my own. If I tell you I love you, you've got me. You will lay all kinds of expectations on me, and I will have no freedom left. When I protest, you will say, "Well, you told me you loved me. Don't you?" Some boys experienced their mothers that way, and have been on guard ever since. They keep their distance, fearing they will get caught again in what they call "that bottomless pit of emotional need." They don't give their wives anything on their birthdays. They won't be tied down to being home at a certain time. They avoid saying "I love you." Many women are similarly afraid of being swallowed up, of becoming Mrs. So-and-So and playing the role of revolving satellite, of getting pulled into a life dedicated to meeting someone else's needs. They fear having no money, no mind, no voice, no freedom.

3. I will be shattered if I lose what I love. Far safer not to love anyone or anything too much, for loss is total devastation. Those of us who as children lost a parent through death or divorce know this devastation feelingly. Anyone who has formed a close bond of love later in life and then been rejected knows how shattering that is. Once having had such an experience we often vow unconsciously that we will never let ourselves get that close again. A man and his wife on the verge of divorce sought counseling. It was the man's second marriage. In the course of the conversation, it came out that his first wife had left him for someone else. Deeply wounded by the rejection, he said he made a *conscious* decision at that time: "I will never give myself completely away again. I will always hold something in reserve." But it didn't work. His second wife was divorcing him because he had never really been there.

4. I have never experienced intimacy, and I simply don't know how to get close. Some people want closeness, but are at a loss how to proceed. Others were so deeply hurt early by parental rejection that they move through life with a sort of distant numbness, neither contemplating nor aspiring to intimacy. These must come to know through the experience of someone caring for them that there is such a thing as interpersonal bonding, and then they have to learn gradually how to deepen it.

So How Do You Get Close?

The answer is, the same way porcupines make love— very, very carefully. And it takes two people working together. Either can arrest the development.

1. Make a decision that you will seek and open yourself to intimacy, even though it entails hurts along the way, even though it sets you up for the pain of loss. This decision is foundational, more important than any skills of intimacy that you might learn. The opposite decision, which may not even be fully conscious, is the greatest block to intimacy. Why would a sensible person choose intimacy when it entails such great risks? Because we are made for love. Love is the highest possibility of our nature, the reason for our creation. Nothing else satisfies; nothing else gives our lives a purpose that is worthy of us. As Alfred Lord Tennyson said: "It is better to have loved and lost than never to have loved at all." There are, of course, many ways to love, many levels of involvement with others. Among them, there seems to be no love quite as challenging and growthful as real intimacy with another individual.

When we take marriage vows, we give the gift of ourself to the other person for life. It is one thing to say the words. It is another actually to give the gift. We give something of it when we serve each other, something again when we give our bodies. But there is a huge part of it we do not give if we hold back our inner self. We know the value of *that* gift if anyone has ever given it to us. We are touched by their trust, admire their courage, and feel reverence for what has been entrusted. For when we receive the gift of the inner self, we instinctively feel we are in the presence of the holy.

2. Push yourself across your threshold of comfort, and share what feels dangerously personal. It might be asking for what you enjoy sexually. It might be sharing something from your childhood that was traumatic for you and has left its emotional mark. It might be disclosing what you struggle with deep inside right now, e.g., feelings of inadequacy, of disappointment in yourself, of a loss of direction. It might be sharing a victory you feel you are winning against something you have battled in yourself for a long time. Letting ourselves be known in risk-taking ways is half the process by which we get close. The other half is being the kind of receiver who allows the other to unfold in a space safe enough so that they can come close too.

The following dialogue took place between a newly married couple.

George: I know we both care about each other, but I feel like our relationship is superficial. You don't share your feelings with me. Like about your work. You never talk about how you feel about your work.

Cathy: That's because I don't feel good about my work. I feel very inadequate (starts to cry). It feels OK to share it with my therapist because it's a very contained situation, and I think she can help me with it. But I'm afraid to share it with you. I think it would just burden you, and you would probably think less of me too (cries some more).

George: (Gently) I feel closer to you already, just because you've told me this much. I see how much pain you are carrying. That's why I want to know about it. I don't want to be your therapist. I don't want to try to solve it either. I just want to walk side by side with you.

Cathy: But isn't it just going to add to your burdens?

George: Maybe so, in a way. But I want to be able to share my burdens with you, too, and I don't want to depress you. Isn't that what marriage is all about, two people sharing each other's burdens—and each other's joys too?

Cathy: Yes, you're right. I see how important it is. It's still hard for me though. I've always been independent, and this is very new. But I see the importance of it, and I will try to share more with you.

3. Keep your fear of rejection more manageable by starting with smaller, less threatening items. Start with small steps, with personal material that pushes you across your threshold but still does not put you *too* much at risk. You need to gain the experience that you can let yourself be known and still be safe. And you need to enjoy the good feeling that comes with increased closeness to be motivated to venture further. Work your way gradually from the less to the more vulnerable, bit by bit, over time. Let your mate know this is difficult for you and ask for patience.

4. Work on your partner a bit, if necessary, to help them be the kind of receiver you need. Closeness is a relationship, and it requires two. You may need to encourage your mate to show more interest in what goes on inside of you, or to listen without interrupting, or to ask more questions to draw you out, or to refrain from evaluating or trying to solve what you are sharing, or to be sure to keep what you are saying to themselves. Ask for what you need.

5. Protect yourself from getting swallowed up by asserting yourself and by setting limits at appropriate points. Asserting yourself means saying what you think or feel or want, even if it is different from what your mate thinks or feels or wants. That is how you remain your own person. Setting limits at appropriate points means refusing your mate's requests sometimes, because to say yes would be to lose yourself in a way you are not comfortable with. You might say no to getting up and making your mate's breakfast. You might say no to sex at times. You might say no to a request to be at home to an extent that seems stifling to you. Particularly if your mate has fairly strong dependency needs, you will need to assert yourself and set limits quite a bit, or you *will* be swallowed up and lose yourself. And that would not be growthful for either of you. But this kind of appropriate limit-setting is very different from deciding not to be close so as to avoid the struggle entirely, or deciding never to say, "I love you," lest your mate try to stake a claim on it.

It is always possible to get closer in marriage, even when we have been married for years and years. We keep changing, so there is always more to disclose. We mellow, too, so that previously impossible topics become by God's graciousness possible. Some of these deeper things inside of us need the right time and place to come out. Couples who take care to create those more open times and more conducive settings usually reap a rich reward in increased intimacy.

EXERCISE 2: MARITAL INTIMACY INVENTORY

Read through these descriptions of the kinds of intimacy that deepen a marriage relationship. Then take time for you and your spouse each to choose the one area where you are most satisfied with your relationship, and the area where you would most like to see your relationship grow. Share your selections with one another. Throughout the book you will find suggestions for developing these aspects of your marriage.

____ 1. *Commitment Intimacy:* A sense of being "for" each other, trust, investment in the ongoing growth of the relationship.

____ 2. *Emotional Intimacy:* Sharing of significant meanings and feelings, the touching of the innermost selves of two human beings.

____ 3. ***Sexual Intimacy:*** Sensual-emotional satisfaction, the experience of physical sharing, pleasure, fun.

____ 4. ***Intellectual Intimacy:*** Sharing the world of ideas, reading, discussing, studying.

____ 5. ***Aesthetic Intimacy:*** Sharing experiences of beauty—music, nature, art, theater, dance, movies.

____ 6. ***Creative Intimacy:*** Sharing in acts of creating together, parenting and other ventures, mutually feeding each other so that each can realize his/her potentialities as a person.

____ 7. ***Recreational Intimacy:*** Relating in experiences of fun and play.

____ 8. ***Work Intimacy:*** The closeness of sharing common tasks, such as maintaining a house and yard, raising a family, earning a living.

____ 9. ***Crisis Intimacy:*** Closeness in coping with problems and pain, standing together in the major and minor tragedies of life.

____ 10. ***Service Intimacy:*** Shared dedication to a common cause or value beyond the marriage.

____ 11. ***Spiritual Intimacy.*** Sharing life meanings, faith, forgiveness, expressions of worship, awe, wonder.

____ 12. ***Communication Intimacy:*** Shared vulnerability through mutual self-disclosure, receptive listening, acceptance and feedback.

____ 13. ***Conflict Intimacy:*** Facing and working through differences to creative resolution and increased closeness.

____ 14. ***Intimacy and Autonomy:*** Respect for the natural rhythm of intimacy and aloneness, accepting each other's needs for privacy and solitude.

Chapter 3
Communicating Well

———— ◇ ————

If we were asked to name the single most important ingredient in a successful marriage, the core skill on which everything else hinges, we would choose communication. For, more than anything else, marriage is a long conversation.

The conversation ranges over a great many topics: managing the details of daily living, making plans, letting needs and wants be known, commenting on what is going on in the life of the larger world, getting into conflict and trying to resolve it, reaching decisions together, sharing what is deep in the heart. All of this is communication.

Human beings communicate in many ways. The most obvious way is through words. But we also communicate by silence, by tone of voice and volume, by facial and bodily expression. We communicate by leaving, or by not showing up, or by coming late. But we communicate through words more than in any other way, and some ways of doing that are more constructive than others—more likely, that is, to result in satisfaction for both parties. The following are some guidelines, culled from experts who have studied human communication very closely, for making our exchanges as constructive as possible. There will be further refinements in the chapters on "Managing Anger Constructively," and "Negotiating Conflict." But first, the most basic guidelines.

1. *Listen without interrupting.* All of us want to be heard. It actually saves time to listen rather than to interrupt and respond prematurely. That way you get the message, and it is the message that you respond to. The main reason people keep repeating themselves in endless arguments is that they still feel they have not been heard. Listen respectfully. Listen carefully. Listen for the feelings within the words. Listen for the deeper issue, a concern more general and more important than the specific item under discussion.

2. *Check to be sure you have the message before you respond to it.* "Let me see if I understand what you're saying," is the way to start, and then play the message back to check for your accuracy of understanding. Your mate will often have some correction. But now you've really got the message. This guideline is important because it is amazing how partial our hearing often is, and how easily we distort—especially if we are working on our reply instead of listening.

3. *Agree before you disagree.* When it is your turn to speak, don't start with "But." Start with "Yes." That is, agree as far as you can before you disagree. That is what makes your mate feel heard and taken seriously. *Then* you can differ where you differ, and *you* will have a much better chance of being heard. Here is an example of what not to do, followed by an example of a more effective approach.

> *Amy:* I'm still angry with you because the other night when I told you how I think I've really

come to a breakthrough in my job and am starting to feel good about myself finally, you weren't even listening to me! This is the most important thing that has happened to me for years, and you are supposed to be my best friend. But when I try to share this with you, all the while I'm talking, you've got one eye on some TV program! (She tears up.)

John: Listen. I already told you, don't try to talk to me when I am watching TV. Am I supposed to be tuned in to you all the time, ready to drop everything and just listen to you?

Amy: This is exactly what I'm talking about. I don't mean a thing to you! I'm telling you about the most important thing in my life, and you'd rather watch TV.

This conversation is going nowhere. John began by disagreeing instead of agreeing, which just made Amy angrier. Now the couple is really polarized. Let's run it again.

Amy: (Exactly as above.)

John: You're right. I really was distracted, and I'm sorry. I know how important this is to you, and it's very important to me too. I think your breakthrough is wonderful, and I want to talk with you more about it. (He takes her hand.)

But can I say something about the other night? When you brought it up, I really was im-

mersed in that program. It just wasn't a good setting for talking about something that important.

John has a valid point: Amy chose a poor moment. But
this time he does not *begin* with his defense; he begins by
agreeing with her. She feels heard, validated. So now she
has some good will for considering *his* point of view.

4. Take just one issue at a time. If you take more than
one, you won't settle any of them. You and your mate
will just range all over the place, and nothing will be
resolved. And the point is to reach some kind of closure
on the issue that is raised. That demands staying with it.
So you yourself have to resist going down interesting side
roads (sometimes escape routes), and if your mate does it,
all you have to say is, "OK, let's come back to the main
issue." You have to keep it focused if you want to get
anywhere.

**5. Talk mainly about yourself in the relationship; maxi-
mize I-statements rather than You-statements.** Talk
more about what goes on inside you than about what
you think is going on with the other person. This is
harder than it sounds. It seems to come more naturally
to us to talk about the other person, in critical terms:
"You're so . . . !" "You always . . . !" But it is a great deal
more constructive to talk about what goes on inside us
in relation to the other's behavior. Some examples will
make this clear.

Rob and Nancy are driving home from a party. Nancy
says to him with an edge in her voice: "I couldn't believe
how much you monopolized the conversation tonight."
Or she might be even more accusatory: "How come you
always have to be the center of attention?" Either way,
she is talking much more about Rob than about herself.
Whether she goes with the statement or the question, he

will feel attacked and will most likely respond defensively. From here, they will most likely move into a bout of accusation and denial.

Suppose she talked about her feelings instead, saying something like this: "It really bothers me when I see you talking so much more than anyone else at a party." Now she is simply sharing what she feels in relation to a certain outward behavior. She is not telling him what he is trying to do or what his motives are, which would be mind reading. She simply names the behavior, without judging it, and let's Rob know that it bothers her. There is a request implied, that he stop talking so much and give others a chance to say more, possibly including herself. But her statement of feeling is open enough to allow their discussion to move as easily in the other direction, inviting her to examine why she is so bothered by this behavior. Maybe *she* has a problem. And maybe that is why we would rather not talk mainly about ourselves. It is a lot easier just to judge the other person.

Having an argument in which each of us is simply trying to win is very different from having an argument in which each of us is trying to listen for the truth. When we do that, we are in the spiritual realm, for the truth might require that we abandon our original position and even change longstanding behavior. To be subject to the truth in this way is to submit our egos to a higher claim, which is ultimately to be subject to God.

In a kitchen in another house, Mary and Steve are talking about Mary's purchase yesterday of a $99 dress. It is Steve who speaks, and he sounds angry. "You have an uncanny ability to go out and blow a bundle of money exactly when we can least afford it." Or he could focus his attack more specifically: "You've got a whole closet full of clothes, yet there you go again out to buy something else. You have absolutely no sense of financial responsibility." In either case, it is Mary, not himself, that he is talking about, and he is obviously putting her in the wrong.

Suppose he were to talk about himself more, and specifically about his feelings. "I'm really upset about that dress you bought yesterday. Can we talk about it?" This statement opens a touchy discussion but in a less threatening way. It shares information about what is going on inside Steve. He seems willing to examine his own subjectivity rather than to make supposedly objective statements about her.

In sum, talk mainly about yourself rather than about your mate, and talk about your feelings in relation to your mate's outwardly observable behavior. Don't try to guess what their motives might be, because you don't really know. And don't talk about "reality" as if you saw it objectively.

6. Talk mainly about feelings rather than about thoughts. Somehow our feelings tell more about us than our ideas do. An example of this is being with a very intellectual person, listening to their ideas for some time, perhaps even taking a whole course from them, and coming away with very little sense of who they really are. We have no *feel* for them, no sense of what their humanity is. If, by contrast, someone talks about what they like and don't like, what they value and are interested in, what some of their experiences have been and how they have felt about them, we come away with much more of a sense of who they are. One measure of how much feeling you are sharing is how vulnerable you feel. Sharing our knowledge does not make us very vulnerable; sharing our feelings does.

7. *When you talk about your position, use expressions like "I think" and "It seems to me".* This is to own and acknowledge your subjectivity. What the truth of matters is, it is very hard to say. All we have is the way we see it and what we think about it. "I just think a woman's place is in the home," is one of those nice subjective statements almost anyone can accept—as your opinion. It beats "A woman's place is in the home," uttered as an objective truth. If we can recognize how subjective all of our views are, how conditioned by our peculiar life history, we are in a much better position to understand and accept other people's subjectivity too, and to be flexible in negotiating.

8. *When you talk about your mate, use "seems" and "sometimes."* "Sometimes" and "not very often" are much easier to listen to than "always" and "never," which are exaggerations. "You never say you love me," will probably put your mate on the defensive and get the response: "I do too," and they can probably give you an instance. "You always put me down," will evoke a similar response: "I do not." "Sometimes" and "not very often" are not only more accurate; they are less inflammatory, and will probably open a more constructive discussion of the matter. Similarly, "seems" is much truer to our subjective impressions of others than are bald statements of fact. "You seem angry," is much better than "You're angry." "You seem down," is much better than "You're depressed." "You don't seem to be listening," is much better than "You're not listening." Most people do not appreciate being told what is going on inside them.

9. *Express the positive freely.* We don't have to praise one another as if we were perfect. There is no call for saying anything we do not genuinely mean. But there is

so much room for the expression of affirmation, appreciation, and thanks.

> You look terrific!
> You have a wonderful sense of humor.
> Thanks for doing the dishes (the wash, the
> vacuuming, etc.)
> You're great with kids.
> You've always been an excellent provider.
> That was great sex.
> You're still my favorite person.
> You were in terrific form at the party tonight.
> Thanks for making those calls.
> That was a wonderful presentation you gave.
> I love you.

Remarks like these do not cost anything. They carry no
penalty. They never sound old, no matter how many
times they are said. They oil the machinery, revive the
spirit, increase the closeness. And they have an excellent
chance of bringing on more good behavior. When we express our joy in our mate, we express something of the joy
God takes in them. And this kind of appreciation is just
as vital to their growth as caring confrontation.

10. Express the negative too, but do it respectfully. The
negative needs to be expressed in an intimate relationship, too, because irritations and disappointments unaddressed gradually increase distance. The Christian ideal
is not to avoid hurting anyone's feelings, but to tell the
truth with love.

So why do we hesitate to express the negative? Sometimes it is because we don't want to hurt our mate's
feelings. What we fail to realize is that the distant silence
will hurt their feelings too. So will the angry explosion

when we can't hold it in anymore. We might hesitate to express the negative because we are afraid our spouse will get mad and attack us. They might. Then we may have to resort to another guideline: "OK, I hear you, but let's take one issue at a time." The *way* we express the negative will have a lot to do with the kind of response we get. Our general guideline for how to express it is given just above: Express how you feel in relation to outwardly observable behavior.

Finally, the sort of general climate we establish together as a couple has much to do with how it goes when we express negative feelings. If we are compassionate, we are much more likely to be treated with compassion. And if we habitually express the positive, creating a loving atmosphere, the negative will not be so hard to take.

EXERCISE 3: TIME-LIMITED INTERCOMMUNICATION

In his book, *Marital Myths*, Arnold Lazarus says that the following technique has worked wonders with many couples who were willing to use it regularly.

Set aside three, separate, half-hour-long appointments with each other every week for the next month. These sessions are to be taken very seriously and must be viewed as high priorities. Ideally, to derive the greatest benefit from this exercise you need five things—a quiet room where you will not be interrupted, an automatic timer, pencil, paper, and a coin.

Flip the coin to determine who talks first. Set the timer for five minutes. During these five minutes the talker discusses whatsoever he or she pleases. *The listener may not interrupt.* He or she may take notes in preparation for clarification or response, but no verbal output is to occur until the five minutes elapse and the bell rings (unless the other person does not require the full five minutes and says "I'm through for now").

When the timer goes off, the talker is to stop immediately whatever he or she is saying. At that point the listener paraphrases (repeats back the essence of) the speaker's message. If the speaker is not satisfied with the listener's playback, he or she says, "You haven't got it quite right," and repeats that part of the message. The listener paraphrases again and again until the speaker is fully satisfied. Once the speaker feels that he/she has been fully listened to and understood, he/she says "That's right," or "Thank you, you heard me." The timer is set for another five minutes, with the previous listener now doing the talking under the same ground rules.

In a typical half-hour session, each person usually has two separate five-minute opportunities to speak. If the paraphrases are brief and accurate, couples may take a few extra minutes and each have three talking and listening periods. At the end of the session, it is important to hug each other and to drop any further discussion of the issues that were raised until the next preset appointment.

Chapter 4

Managing Anger Constructively

―――――――― ◇ ――――――――

One of the early surprises of our own marriage was how different our anger styles were. Kathy's anger would flash as soon as I did something that bothered her. She would tell me in no uncertain terms just how she felt about it, voice raised, face intense. At first I would wilt, as I had little preparation for this. In my family, anger was held in. If somebody *did* blow up, it was a really big deal, a family crisis. In her family, by contrast, anger was frequent and free; it flashed and passed, a normal part of daily life. This has taken some getting used to on my part. But Kathy has had a corresponding difficulty in dealing with me: she isn't sure when I'm upset. I express my anger by becoming silent and distant. She would much prefer that I come right out with it. We are both products of our family cultures, and culture is hard to shake. Yet we have noticed over the years of our marriage that the edge of her anger has softened, and that I have become more aware and expressive when I am angry. So we have had a good effect on one another. But you would still notice a clear difference in our styles.

Anger is the most difficult emotion to deal with in marriage, as it is in relationships generally. Nice people wish it just were not there. But anger is inevitable in intimate relationships, because closeness brings us up against our differences, and differences are both frustrating and threatening.

For all the difficulty it poses, anger serves a very useful purpose in life. It gives us both information and energy. It informs us that we feel somehow threatened or unhappy in a situation; and it makes energy available for making the change we need to make in order to be comfortable again. Every animal organism is endowed with anger for its own protection. It is the vital power behind fight or flight. In humans, it is the energy that fuels many of the great social movements, the power behind the dedication to removing injustice and needless suffering. So anger is basically a good thing, an emotion in the service of life-preservation and life-enhancement. There is nothing immoral about it. The moral issue is to manage it well, to use it constructively rather than destructively, for, like all human energies, it can do good or evil.

The Problem with Venting Anger

When someone gives anger full vent, it becomes a surge of power sweeping the person along. Anything can erupt: shouting, abusive talk, throwing things, pushing and shoving, punching, killing. There is a feeling of exhilaration in the person so swept away and free of all restraint, a wonderful feeling of power, a deeply satisfying vindication. But there are victims too—property and persons. Human relationships cannot sustain much of this kind of thing. Such behavior is either the end of the relationship, with bitter feelings and a very real danger of revenge; or it is the symptom of a seriously sick ongoing situation.

Fortunately, for the vast majority of married couples it is not this bad. But those who are inclined to vent their anger, even if they do it far less dramatically, need to look at what their behavior is doing.

Stan and Valerie were a couple who both had strong tempers. They loved and enjoyed each other much of the time. But when something set either of them off, it became an entirely different situation. The offended party would blow up and say something abusive to the other, who would take it as a sign of war. He or she would reply in kind. Voices were raised, neither would listen, exaggerated statements were made, past offenses were dragged in, vile language and name-calling were freely indulged in. It was attack and counterattack, with clear intent to hurt.

Then would come the silence—and the silence would last for days. Each had plenty of capacity for stubbornness, and would wait for the other to apologize. Neither would do it. This would go on for anywhere from three to eight days. It was an endurance contest, to see who would break down first, as they ate at the same table, slept in the same bed, read the paper or watched TV in the same living room day after day. Finally one of them would apologize, or one would make some humorous remark and know from the response that the climate had changed, and they would gradually work their way back to some measure of closeness. But they would not discuss the original incident or issue for fear of starting it up again. So nothing got resolved, and it was just a matter of time before the next eruption.

This pattern of behavior took its toll. Besides the pure waste of all the days they spent in the loneliness and discomfort of cold war, there was the damage to trust, the hurt of the names and harsh judgments that stuck in the mind, the growing difficulty of sexual relating. Theirs was a marriage filled with hazard.

What this couple is wrestling with is at bottom a spiritual issue, because it so clearly carries a call to a change of heart. The behavior they regularly exhibit is unloving and destructive. Intimacy has brought them up against their sinfulness and woundedness, presenting them with a challenge and opportunity for healing and growth. The growth would consist not in eliminating anger, which is impossible, but in learning to *manage* it in a much more loving way.

The Problem with Suppressing Anger

If venting anger is not constructive, neither is suppressing it. The person who suppresses anger, more often a woman than a man, was probably taught by her parents that anger is bad, particularly for girls, and she never saw her parents, or at least her mother, express it. This was perhaps reinforced by a spirituality which taught that anger is morally wrong and should always be replaced by love. So she holds it in, sometimes even denying that it exists.

Yet anger does exist and stir in her—when she is hurt, frustrated, or threatened. It always somehow expresses itself outwardly, too, though in her case this is not in the form of loud words or aggressive actions. It comes out as tears, or as silence, or as withdrawal, or as avoidance, or as withholding. If it came to any verbal expression, the words might be: I'm disappointed, or I'm sad, or I just wish. . . . These are some of anger's more polite disguises.

When anger exists but is denied, it exacts a high price of our inner life. The price is depression. For when anger is not directed outward to the offender, or used as signal and energy for changing our situation, it usually turns inward and eats away at us as depression. So if we find ourselves depressed, a good question to ask ourselves is: Whom am I angry at?

If we are inclined to suppress anger, the skills we need to learn are first awareness, then assertiveness. First we must peel away anger's disguises so that we are no longer fooling ourselves. Then we have to share our anger with the person who is bothering us, or, if that does not seem possible or constructive, do something to take better care of ourselves. Then we have made good use of it and can enjoy the relief. Unpleasant as anger is either to feel or to listen to, it does carry this opportunity.

The habit of suppressing anger is a spiritual issue too. For it is usually rooted in low self-esteem. We need to grow into the recognition of our own dignity and worth, and own that our needs and wants are just as worthy of consideration as anybody else's. Jesus' injunction was, "Love your neighbor as you love *yourself.*" When we begin to love ourselves, we then need *courage* as we make our needs known, risking others' surprise or disapproval. These are difficult but wonderful spiritual victories for the self-effacing pleaser.

Working Anger through Together

To make anger work for you instead of against you in your marriage, you might find the following guidelines helpful:

1. Acknowledge it. Don't deny it. Don't minimize it. Reflect on what it means, and decide what you want to do with it. You might decide not to express it because it is no big deal, or because you recognize it is your problem more than your mate's. Or you might decide not to express it because you have done that many times before and it has done no good. But if that is the case, think about what you *will* do with it. Since you cannot change your mate, how can you change *your* role in the interaction so that the two of you don't just keep going around and around in the same frustrating way?

2. *Express your anger without venting.* It is crucial to recognize that even those of us who have "bad tempers" have a *choice* about how we will express the anger we feel. We may be very much in the *habit* of expressing anger abusively, and our reactions feel automatic and un-stoppable. Yet we do not behave this way when we feel anger, for example, toward our customers, our boss, or strangers we know could hurt us. That means we can control it; we do have a choice. Men's anger-management groups all insist on this principle as foundational:

> We choose to be abusive; we can choose not to be.
> We have learned to be abusive; we can learn not to be.

It may take some time for us to change our habits, but we do have a choice. We make that choice out of respect for our mate and our children. It means no long tirades, no physical violence of any kind, no name-calling, no defamation of character.

3. *Share the feelings that lie beneath the anger.* Anger is a reflex emotion. It is aroused by feelings that occur first, and these are hurt, frustration, or fear. Anger is a hard emotion with a lot of energy behind it, because its function is to defend the threatened organism. Hurt, frustration, and fear are tender, vulnerable emotions. When we share them, our voices are soft and we might even have tears in our eyes. These emotions are much easier for our partner to listen to than the hard edge of our anger, and they much more readily provoke a caring response. They are also much more informative. Of course, sharing the tender feelings beneath the anger makes us more vulnerable, and so it is harder to do. But the jewel the effort yields is more truth and greater intimacy.

4. When your partner is expressing anger, listen awhile before you speak. Anger is no fun to listen to, but it tells you that your partner is hurting about something. He or she needs most of all to have a sense that you care about that. The best way to show it is to listen. Don't interrupt. Don't jump in to defend yourself. These responses just fan the flames. If you listen, and then acknowledge that your partner has some point, his or her anger usually abates considerably right away. Then you can share your point of view.

5. If one or both of you are very hot, call time out. This is basic damage control. Make a general agreement that if either of you thinks anger is at a risky level, that person can call or signal a time out, which the other will accept without any further words. Go apart awhile if possible, to take the time you need to cool down and to think things over. But the person who called the time out has the obligation to bring the matter back for resolution, and to do it within a reasonable time.

6. Become aware of and do something about the remote causes of your anger. If you find yourself getting angry a lot even over relatively trivial matters, there is probably a deeper unhappiness which has you at a high threshold of irritability. You may be unhappy with your work or with the general direction of your life. You may be under stress from troubling external events. You may have deeper levels of dissatisfaction with your marriage. Or you might be exhausted and in need of a break or an unloading of some of the demands you are trying to meet. Frequent crying

spells are a similar indication of this deeper level of unhappiness; often tears are the expression of anger. Making
the basic changes you need to make in your life, and
taking good care of yourself generally, are the best prepara-
tions for handling life's irritations with good grace.

7. ***Work through unresolved childhood issues that may
still have you angry.*** Sometimes the best way to go forward is to go back. When you find your angry reactions to
certain situations are way out of proportion, you are
probably dealing with rage from the past, and you need to
get at the original events which caused the deep hurt
which still abides. We say more about this in the chapter
on "Recognizing the Power of the Past."

EXERCISE 4: PROCESSING ANGER AS A COUPLE

In *Love and Anger in Marriage,* David and Vera Mace
describe a three-step plan that they developed for dealing
with anger in their own marriage. They say this way of
processing anger—though not easy and at first calling for
a good deal of work—made a marked difference in the
quality of their marriage. See if their procedure will work
for you.

1. Make an agreement that you will communicate your
states of anger to each other as soon as possible, and
before they lead to harmful consequences. Accept as perfectly normal the fact that you will from time to time get
angry with each other, and give each other permission to
do so. This clears the air and frees you from guilt.

2. Make a pledge to each other that while it is OK to be
angry, it is not OK to attack the other in anger. This
agreement provides a valuable safeguard, and frees you

from any need to develop retaliatory anger and launch a counterattack.

3. Make a contract that every anger situation that occurs in your relationship will be owned and worked through by both of you, not as a personal weakness in the one who is angry, but as a function of your total relationship. In step three, the angry person requests help, and the one toward whom the anger is being directed gives assurance of a response. Anger can be processed positively only by both acting together.

Chapter 5
Negotiating Conflict

———— ◇ ————

Men and women are attracted to each other because they are different and hence fascinating to each other. As Ashleigh Brilliant says: "No wonder I'm confused; one of my parents was a man, the other a woman." And the differences do not end with gender. There are countless other differences of experience and personality besides.

It is not long before the differences that initially attracted begin to repel. I was fascinated by your exuberance of feeling; now I wish you would use your mind once in a while. I loved your cool rationality, your deliberation and imperturbability; now you seem terribly controlled and controlling. It was your spontaneity and free play that first drew me to you; today I find you awfully irresponsible. It was your shyness, your silence, your mystery that lured me; now I'm tired of living with a stranger. You once seemed so admirably frugal, so careful in every purchase; my, you seem tight to me now!

Forgetting that all these qualities are good and continue to contribute to the richness of living with this particular person, we somehow get focused on their downside and go to work trying to change our mate. We get angry, criticize, plead for change, suggest they get counseling, fantasize other partners, threaten to leave. Very little changes—except that we become more and more exhausted. For *we cannot change or control an-other person.* Hard truth. But saving truth, in the sense that it will save us years of frustration if we accept it. We can *ask* that they change something, but only they can do the changing, and they have to be both willing and able to do it.

They may be unwilling, for good reasons. They may be unable, or at least severely limited in their ability to change some things. In any case, that is their business, not ours. The only person we can change is ourself—and that, as we know, is not easy. How many years have we been trying to change certain things about ourselves, and how far have we gotten? This should at least make us compassionate.

One of the first questions we have to ask is, *should* there be a change? There is a wonderful little story in Eastern mysticism about a palace prime minister who, in his tour of the palace grounds one day, saw a falcon for the first time in his life. Thinking it a very strange sort of pigeon, he took a knife and trimmed its claws, its wings, and its beak. The task completed, he felt satisfied that he had done what the keeper of birds had somehow failed to do.

We have three basic options when we don't like the situation we are in: 1) We can try to get some change. (We can *ask* for it. Or we can simply change what *we* are doing in the situation that allows it to remain the way it is.) 2) We can accept things the way they are and try not to let them bother us so much. (This, too, is basically a change in ourselves, inner rather than outer.) 3) We can leave the situation. The first option is usually the most appealing, and that is what this chapter is about.

Bob and Carol had a long go-around on the matter of cleanliness and order. Bob had higher standards, stemming from the fact that he had grown up in a house kept very tidy by an ever-vigilant mother. He felt instant irritation when he came home from work and found the house "a mess." He had tried many, many times to get Carol to keep the place the way he wanted it kept. Carol had grown up in a home in which neatness was a much lower priority, and she did not even notice the things that bothered Bob so much. She kept trying to sell Bob on the idea that their home was a space to *live* in, and that what was important was that family members could relax at home, enjoy the place, and enjoy each other. She enjoyed it the way it was; why couldn't he? Bob said he could not relax there when the living room had papers and clothes strewn around, the bathroom needed cleaning, and everything was dusty. This had been a years-long argument, even though with considerable goodwill Bob had tried many times not to let the situation bother him so much, while Carol had made efforts to make the house look the way Bob wanted it to.

The form the battle takes here, as often, is that the person with higher standards categorically says to the other, "I want you to do it, but I want you to do it my way." Bob tries to control Carol; Carol, naturally, resists being controlled. The arena of battle here is neatness, but it can just as well be finances, parenting, jobs, or anything else. I want you to manage our finances—but the way I would. I want you to deal with the repair people—but the way I would. If you want to succeed at your job, do it my way.

To resolve a tug of war of this kind, it must first be agreed that both person's approaches are probably legitimate; they are just *different*. This is hard to grant, so wedded are we to the rightness of our positions, yet it is almost always true. Then, the general principle is that if it is really important to us that something be done and that it be done a certain way, we must do it ourselves; and that if we want someone else to do it and they agree, we must let them do it their way.

And so, with a little coaching along these lines, Bob and Carol made a deal. Bob selected the household tasks which were most important to him and took responsibility for them himself. These were the bathrooms, the dusting, the windows, and the linoleum floors. Her tasks thus made more manageable, Carol agreed to make the beds every day, to put dirty dishes in the dishwasher after each meal and to empty it when the dishes were done, and to vacuum once a week. That pretty well took care of it. The one item that continued to be a source of irritation was newspapers, shoes, etc., lying around the house. The way they agreed to handle it was that, since Carol did not usually notice such things, Bob would simply pick up and put away what was bothering him. And as far as the kids rooms were concerned, they agreed that each of their kids could keep their rooms as they saw fit, but they had to keep their doors closed.

All this may sound fairly simple and obvious, but it takes most couples a long time to come to an agreement of this kind, if indeed they ever come to it. The reasons are:

1. They keep arguing as if one is right and one is wrong. Of course, neither is willing to admit that they are wrong. They need to reframe the entire argument into one about legitimate *differences* which are neither right nor wrong.

2. One or both keep thinking if they just push hard enough, they will eventually get all they want. They need to start thinking in terms of compromise.

3. Each just keeps repeating their positions. Neither takes it a step further and makes a concrete proposal for a solution.

4. If a proposal is made and rejected, no counterproposal is offered. So the matter remains unresolved, just waiting for the next blowup. They need to keep brainstorming possible solutions and modifying rough ideas until they have an agreement they can both live with.

5. One fails to keep the agreement made, and the other takes that as permission to stop doing what they agreed to. If a couple wants to make progress toward the resolution of their problems, each needs to take extreme care to keep the agreements they work so hard to reach. And if one falls down, this is not license for the other to give the whole thing up. Some failures are to be expected as each works to change old habits.

Don and Cheryl had a long-standing sexual conflict. Don loved sex, and wanted to have it every day. Cheryl couldn't understand his fascination. For her, sex was all right once in a while, but it would not have greatly bothered her if for any reason they simply had to do without it. She loved hugs almost anytime, and enjoyed some physical intimacy in bed before they slept. "I just like to be held," she said. "The genital rigamarole I can do without." But she had discovered that it was dangerous to hug Don, or to be physically affectionate with him in bed, because he took everything as a come-on and there was no way to calm him down again. So Cheryl more and more avoided all physical contact, and submitted to sex only on rare occasions. She thought Don was oversexed and needed therapy. He thought she had hangups and needed therapy. When both were weary of the battle, they came for therapy together.

Here is the compromise they worked out. Don and

Cheryl would have sex twice a week as a general expectation, once on the weekend and once during the week. Cheryl would initiate at least one of those, and could initiate twice. If she initiated twice, Don would not initiate that week. Either could refuse the other's initiative, but the person who refused incurred the obligation of making the next initiative. They would resume the hugging and the physical intimacy before going to sleep, but Don would never expect or press for anything more unless Cheryl explicitly indicated that she was interested.

This may seem too mechanical or regimented, but it worked for this couple. In terms of frequency, they agreed to meet somewhere between the extremes of his every day and her every month or two. Having a general expectation of twice a week eliminated the problem of his constantly watching his chance and her vigilantly avoiding the slightest sign of affection. They also brought a better balance to their sexual relationship by sharing initiatives equally. Neither got all they wanted. Each made a considerable accommodation to the other's wishes. But the compromise left them both with quite a bit more than they were enjoying before, with the added bonus of peace.

There are, of course, countless small differences in marriage that scarcely require this sort of structured compromise. One of the simplest ways of dealing with them is for either person to say, "OK, let's do it your way," whether it be arranging the furniture this way rather than that, eating out here rather than there, going to this movie rather than that. Good will generally begets good will. When there is rough equality in this give and take, neither party feels resentment, and so neither finds it too hard to give in. It is when one person wants to control almost everything, and the other is tired of being pushed around, that the power struggle is engaged even over tiny matters. A power struggle over a tiny matter is the signal that the *deeper issue* is what needs attention.

Some skills are certainly called for in resolving conflict in marriage, in coming to resolutions that balance both parties' needs and wants in ways that are mutually acceptable. But even more crucial to making and maintaining the peace where there are differences are attitudes that are deeply spiritual—humility and a willingness to examine oneself and change if necessary, reverence for the mystery of the other person and acceptance of them as they are, and generosity in giving. We are not born with these attitudes. They are not usually fully formed even as we enter adulthood, though hopefully we have made some progress toward them. In the "crucible of intimacy" that is marriage, we are provided with many opportunities to expand and deepen them.

EXERCISE 5: THE TRIPLE-INCREASE TECHNIQUE

This is a technique used by many who work with couple enrichment groups. Each partner is asked to make a list of three specific behaviors that they would like the other to *increase*. The requests are expressed in terms of increases rather than decreases so that they will come across more positively.

The requests need to be expressed in terms of *specific* behaviors, not in vague and general terms such as, "I would like you to pay more attention to me," or "I want you to do a better job of communicating." The following examples will give you an idea of the kind of specific behaviors to include.

I want you to increase:

1. The number of times you put down the paper or your book and look at me when we talk.

2. The amount of time you spend helping the kids when they have problems with their homework.

3. The number of days you go jogging or walking with me in the morning.

4. The number of times you pick up the living room without my asking when you see it is messy.

5. The occasions when you talk to my folks on the phone.

After each of you has compiled a list of three behaviors, the next step is to inquire if the specific items are acceptable to the other partner. If not, they have to be modified. When you agree that the requests are reasonable, each partner then indicates a willingness to implement the changes. Some couples prefer to do this as trade-offs, e.g., "If you agree to help the kids with their homework three times a week, I agree to call your folks every Sunday."

Chapter 6

Accepting One Another

—————— ◇ ——————

In the previous chapter we talked about negotiating compromises when significant differences are leading to frustrations. But what do you do when you ask for change and you don't get it, when no compromise seems to be reachable?

Denise and Ron had been married for some twenty-five years and had three children. He was a successful businessman, she a full-time homemaker. He had always been an excellent provider, and one of the ways he had shown his love was to build the family a new home on a lovely hillside, a three-story home with a magnificent view and a large recreation room on the ground floor. Unfortunately, this did not mean a great deal to her because she had back problems and the new house was a lot more trouble than the old, especially with its three stories. Two of the couple's children were off to college now, and the third nearly finished with high school. Denise found herself with a growing unhappiness. What had been a disappointment from the beginning of the marriage had reached a painful acuity in her mind as the child-raising years came to an end: Ron was not much of a soul-mate to her. He never shared his feelings. He came home chattering about his business affairs, and talked freely about other practical matters. But all this held little interest for her. Hers was a world of emotions and of spiritual interests, and he was a very limited companion to her in those realms.

Denise came in for counseling, at a loss what to do. She had moved out, getting an apartment for herself and her youngest son. Her distress was manifesting itself in physical symptoms, as it had from time to time through the years, and she was not sleeping. She knew it had hurt Ron when she moved out, but she felt she could not go on.

At my invitation, Ron joined in the counseling. He was concerned, and seemed genuinely to want to learn the kind of sharing his wife was interested in. But as we worked at it over a series of sessions, I saw that I was not going to be any more successful than she had been at turning him into a sharer of feelings. What feelings he may have had besides his general cheerfulness and optimism, he had no contact with. He lived a simple life of faith, but scarcely pondered its contents. What I saw before me were two good people who loved each other. I could perfectly understand Denise's frustration, but I didn't see how very much could be done about it.

I laid that out for Denise in a session with her alone. "I think you have three basic options," I said. "You could leave Ron and look for a man with a richer emotional and spiritual life who would share that with you. You could resume your marriage with Ron and keep trying to change him, but you haven't gotten very far with that and I haven't been able to either. Or you could resume your marriage with Ron and accept him as he is. But that means letting go of your dream, your dream of what your marriage was supposed to be. And that is nothing less than dying a death." She left with a heavy heart, saying she had to think and pray about all this, and would come back in two weeks.

When she returned, she looked surprisingly serene. "I have some news," she said. "I moved back home." She proceeded to tell me that she had gone through the worst agony of her life for about a week after our last session. She seriously considered leaving Ron, but she couldn't do it. She knew he loved her, and she could not imagine her life without him, nor how he would get along without her. She also saw clearly now that she could not change him, and would have to give up the effort for the sake of her own sanity as well as his. She had just moved back home, to Ron's delight. I told her that I could see in her face and bearing that she had come to a real peace with her decision, difficult as it was, and that I saw in it the possibility of a whole new way of relating to one another. I said I would call her in a month to see how it was going.

When I called, she said things were going well. Ron was working hard as usual, and came home chattering about it as he always had. She was listening to him more now, because she wasn't angry anymore. She had let go. She was spending more time with some women friends who shared her spiritual and emotional interests. She and Ron had started a couple of new activities together: they were taking folk-dancing lessons, and they were going out to the race track once a month or so. "I still feel the sadness sometimes," she said. "I wish it could be deeper between us. But it's all right. Oh, and do you know what Ron did? Shortly after I came back, he said to me that he wants to go to church with me every other Sunday, and we've been doing that. And last week he put the house up for sale!"

Towards a Spirituality of Acceptance

Ron and Denise's story is a tale of gaining by losing. It's a story of dying, and then rising to new life. It brings up one of the central spiritual issues in every marriage. And it illustrates a key psychological point besides. The psychological point is that when we are badgered for love, it is no fun to give it and so we usually don't, because we feel it will never be enough anyway, and who enjoys giving kisses on demand? When our partner lets up, there is both peace and some space for spontaneity. When Denise dropped her campaign to make Ron over, he came forward with gifts of his own. He volunteered to join her in a spiritual activity, and he relinquished *his* dream—their home.

The core spiritual issue that comes into focus here is the issue of acceptance. Every marriage is in some way a mismatch. Nobody gets all they hoped for when they dreamt of their marriage. There is always, even in the best of matches, some sides on which the couple just do not fit well together. It is not very long before that awful fact forces itself upon us, and then what do we do? Leave and marry somebody else? Stay and try to change our partner? Or accept the situation and try to make the most of it?

Loving someone just as they are is always a genuinely spiritual act. Then I am not loving the person for what they might be or do for me, but for what they are in themselves. I am respecting the order of creation, which transcends my particular interests. When I start making people over into what I think they should be, I run the risk of trimming the eagle's beak and clipping its wings.

Jesus was particularly good at loving people just as they were, usually astonishing them by doing so. Each of us knows what a rare and wonderful gift it is when anyone loves us this way. It makes us feel good about our-selves, and that empowers us. When Jesus reached out in this way, people often changed spontaneously, into the best of themselves. Interestingly, it is precisely the kind of love that Jesus had and has for people that as Christian spouses we try to mirror in our marriages. And it is not just imitation that we aspire to. We are trying to be chan-nels or sacraments of his love, so that it can operate *through* us with healing and creative power.

Loving my *spouse* as they are may be the hardest thing of all, because what they are touches me so closely. Such love means dying to dreams of how I thought it should be, how I think I should be loved, what I think would make me happy. These are painful deaths, and so they are simultaneously huge acts of trust in something beyond myself that I believe holds my life with care. Perhaps God's purpose for me is larger than mine, and what God wants to do in me cannot be accomplished in the marriage of my dreams. Perhaps it can be accom-plished only in the marriage I am actually in.

Letting go is not easy. There is a tribe in Africa which captures monkeys by putting food in the bottom of heavy jugs with narrow necks. The monkey smells the food, slips his open hand down the neck of the jug and closes it around the food, then tries to withdraw his hand. He cannot. The hunter easily walks up and captures the monkey—because he won't let go. And so the monkey loses his life. There is a saying of Jesus: "If you try to save your life, you will lose it. But if you lose it freely for my sake, you will find it."

There are some patterns of behavior that should not be accepted because they are destructive of those in the family as well as of the person who perpetrates the behav-ior. Examples would be chronic alcohol or drug abuse, physical violence, sexual abuse. Our talk of acceptance does not apply to these behaviors, but to marriage's non-lethal but very frustrating ordinary differences.

Changing Your Own Behavior in the Interaction

We cannot change or control another person, especially an adult. And in this chapter we advocate loving acceptance of much that vexes us which we cannot change. But this is not to say there is nothing we can do to lessen our distress. As Harriet Lerner points out in *The Dance of Anger*, we can always look at what *we* are doing in the interaction, and change that. This often lessens our feelings of resentment, and sometimes wins a bonus of changed behavior in our mate.

So, for example, I may not be able to get my mate to do more housework, but I can decide that I am going to do less, and say so. If no one picks up the slack, I will live with a less well kept up house. But who knows? Someone may eventually pick up the slack. Similarly, I can tell my too dominant mate that I am seeing the need to make for myself those decisions that most closely touch my life, and make them. My mate may gradually cede control and give me more freedom to make decisions, but even if the attempt to dominate me continues as before, I can resist at certain critical points and decide for myself. In the story with which this chapter begins, Denise changes her steps in the dance when she stops riding Ron for not sharing his feelings and spiritual life, and makes new arrangements for herself to get those needs met elsewhere. Her solution is a nice blend of acceptance and self-care.

This is using the power I have to shape my own destiny. It is very different from those more common attempts to do so which: 1) blame my mate for my unhappiness, 2) try yet again to coerce, manipulate, or cajole them into doing what I want, 3) get into the same old hopeless argument about the matter with shouts, tears, threats, stalking out, or all of the above. The procedure Lerner advocates is rather to figure out where I stand and why, to state it gently but firmly without getting into an argument, and to stick to it with calm resolve in the face of predictable efforts to get me to change back.

Lerner points out that when one person in a relationship overfunctions, the other tends to underfunction, and vice versa. If I do too many household tasks, my mate will probably do few. If I make few decisions, my mate will probably make most of them. If instead of going after my mate to function either more or less than they now do, I change the level of *my own* functioning, it becomes much more difficult for them simply to continue what they were doing. We can be great enablers of what we dislike without realizing the role we are playing in the pattern. But the main goal in changing my part in the pattern is not to change my mate, which may not happen. I have accepted my mate as is. I am simply trying to make my own life better.

Forgiveness

A subcategory of acceptance is forgiveness. For a marriage to stand the test of time, there needs to be a spirit of forgiveness on both sides. We all make mistakes. We do worse than that: we do genuinely evil deeds sometimes. All love of one human being for another is the love of one sinner for another. That is why it requires a spirit of forgiveness and a commitment of fidelity. It is nothing less than God's own love that we embody for each other.

"Forgive and forget" is probably not the best way to state the ideal. We do not forget what impresses us, and hurt impresses us. Forgiving means letting it fade into the past, not holding on to it, not using it against the other person either as a counterblow in a fresh argument or as a justification for my own bad behavior. Forgiveness means it belongs to what is over and done with.

But that immediately suggests a requirement where the offense is concerned. The offense cannot be ongoing. I can forgive a name I was called or a harsh criticism made in a fit of anger even though I was deeply hurt. But am I supposed to forgive this kind of behavior when it happens over and over? Maybe I can forgive a financial blunder that cost us dearly, but am I supposed to forgive an ongoing pattern of financial blundering—or irresponsibility where work is concerned? Maybe I can bring myself to forgive an affair and work painfully toward rebuilding trust and intimacy. But how can I "forgive" an ongoing pattern of infidelity? If bad behavior is ongoing, then the question it raises is not about forgiveness but about acceptance or nonacceptance, which is quite a different matter. Some patterns of behavior are simply not acceptable, even in Christian love.

Forgiveness, when forgiveness is what is called for, is still not easy. We often need God's help to become able to do it. We have to ask God to change our hearts of stone into hearts of flesh, to make fresh blood course through our systems. A step we sometimes need to take is to let our spouse know how much something hurt us before we can forgive it, hopefully getting a heartfelt apology that makes it easier to let go. Apologizing helps a lot, and a spirit of ready apology is probably as crucial as a spirit of forgiveness in maintaining a good marriage.

EXERCISE 6: APPRECIATING OUR DIFFERENCES

When differences become a problem in our relating, we tend to focus on the difficulties they create, and forget the ways in which they enrich our lives. The aim of this exercise is to help us recall the positive side.

Bring to mind qualities in your partner which sometimes irritate you and about which you have sometimes complained. Now see if you can recognize some ways those qualities have also been gifts to you. Surprise your partner by telling them that you appreciate these qualities and why. For example:

> "Your attention to detail, which I sometimes find hard to accept, has saved us from several serious financial errors."

> "Your high energy level, which I resist at times, has gotten us involved in a lot of fun activities and helped us meet new friends."

Chapter 7

Recognizing the Power of the Past

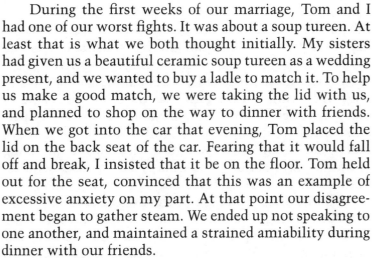

During the first weeks of our marriage, Tom and I had one of our worst fights. It was about a soup tureen. At least that is what we both thought initially. My sisters had given us a beautiful ceramic soup tureen as a wedding present, and we wanted to buy a ladle to match it. To help us make a good match, we were taking the lid with us, and planned to shop on the way to dinner with friends. When we got into the car that evening, Tom placed the lid on the back seat of the car. Fearing that it would fall off and break, I insisted that it be on the floor. Tom held out for the seat, convinced that this was an example of excessive anxiety on my part. At that point our disagreement began to gather steam. We ended up not speaking to one another, and maintained a strained amiability during dinner with our friends.

The next day, when we had calmed down enough to be able to talk about the incident, we tried to figure out why so small an issue had triggered such strong reactions in us. In the process, we learned some interesting things about the way our past family experiences were influencing our relating. Tom acknowledged that the experience had revived memories of his parents' marriage where he saw his dad give in constantly to his mother's demands, to the point where she ran everything. He was determined to avoid a similar pattern, and so had decided to dig in his heels early over any such issues. I discovered that I was afraid marriage would smother a woman's personality and uniqueness. I was fighting for the right to be who I was, even if that wasn't the way Tom thought I should be. Without realizing it, Tom and I were each reacting to patterns rooted in our pasts.

This happens in all marriages. The way we relate is based on what we learned in our original families. They are the source of many of the gifts and strengths we bring to marriage. They are also at the root of some of the things from which we struggle to free ourselves. What happened long ago bestows the blessings and sets the growth tasks for the present marriage. So universal are these patterns that therapist W. Hugh Missildine says in *Your Inner Child of the Past* that there are six people in every marriage bed: the couple and their two sets of parents. Much of this is not in full awareness when we marry, but it comes to awareness through the unfolding of marital interaction. It is usually our spouses who remind us that we are just like our mothers or fathers.

This awareness of the influence of the past may seem to make marriage even more difficult. It is hard enough to relate to one other person, let alone take into account our own and our spouse's complicated pasts. But recognition of how family issues are influencing current relationships isn't meant to add to the difficulties. It can help us deal better with what is already happening, providing insight into puzzling and problematic aspects of our relationships. Further, it is one of the ways in which marriage brings us grace and growth.

The following are some paths to awareness and change in this area.

1. Acknowledge that many of your differences are rooted in the rules and roles of your family cultures. Families have particular ways of doing things, whether that be disciplining children, spending money, or chopping carrots for a salad. The way we learned to do these things while growing up seems familiar; often we declare it to be the only right way. When two people marry, these two different cultures come together, and frequently they collide.

Karen and Peter saw very different approaches to physical affection in their homes. Karen was an only child who never saw her parents touch or kiss one another. They were reserved in their warmth toward her as well. Peter grew up in a large, expressive Italian family, where physical affection flowed freely. He accuses Karen of being uptight and prudish. She resents the warmth he shows to almost all his friends, and becomes jealous when he is freely affectionate with others. She interprets this as a sign that he cares less for her.

Betty notices on visits home that her mom and dad almost never talk to one another directly, but deliver their messages and opinions through her or one of her brothers and sisters. She is disturbed to realize that this is exactly the pattern she and her own husband have established. She had vowed she would not be like her parents, and now finds that she is becoming exactly that. What Karen, Peter, and Betty are discovering is that we tend to return to the familiar, to the only way we have seen things done, even though we might resent that pattern.

Three things are important in making this influence of the past work for our marriage instead of against it. The first is the awareness itself that the rules and roles we hold so strongly stem from patterns in our family of origin. Often this reliance on past needs and patterns is unconscious and automatic. It takes awareness and a conscious choice to begin to change it.

The second helpful step is to stop labeling these differences which stem from family background as right or wrong. We need to see them as evidence of the cultural diversity which results from the way our families saw and did things. When they clash, it is not an opportunity to belittle our spouse and his or her family, but a sign that we need to learn to negotiate the differences.

The third step follows from this, and is one of the ways in which the call to Christian conversion occurs in married life. We must often be willing to compromise, to let go of things that don't matter, and to make changes in ourselves when they do. Karen and Peter, for example, can learn to understand and work with the differences in their approach to affection, each one growing in the process. Betty and her spouse can choose to discontinue past patterns and work toward more direct and honest communication in their marriage. In order to do this, each will have to learn to express their own thoughts and needs clearly.

2. *Notice when you are expecting your mate to meet unexpressed needs that stem from childhood experiences.* Sometimes what we carry from the past is not simply diverse ways of thinking and acting, but unmet needs and expectations. Marriage and family therapist James Framo tells us that none of us ever really gives up the yearning for the love and acceptance of our parents. This yearning underlies the search for other loves and probably lies at the heart of the ecstasy promised by romantic love. When we marry, we are unconsciously looking for healing and wholeness. We choose a spouse hoping that this person will solve the problematic aspects of earlier relationships in our original family. We unconsciously choose a mate who embodies some of the positive and negative traits of our parents, hoping that we will be able to finish our unfinished business with them.

Couples who have been married any length of time begin to recognize that certain arguments get played out time and time again, even if there are slight variations on the themes. These core scenes are repeated over and over, so that we know all the parts almost by heart.

Phil and Marge, who have been married ten years, identified such a core scene as a closeness/distance dance stemming from their family backgrounds. Phil feels smothered by his mother's attention, and resents her attempts to get affection from him. Marge's parents were divorced when she was thirteen, and she thinks of herself as being shuttled from one to the other without a sense that either really wanted her. In their closeness/distance dance, Marge asks for affection and pays lots of attention to Phil's needs, often doing things for him before he can ask. She hopes in this way to get the love she has always needed and wanted. This activates the kind of resentment Phil feels toward his mother's attention. He creates distance the way he saw his father do it in his parents' marriage: he mentions something he knows will be upsetting to Marge and starts an argument.

To change this dynamic in their marriage, Phil and Marge will each have to work on their own issues. Phil needs to take care of the problems with his mother that are troubling his present relationships, and to develop the affectionate aspects of his personality. Marge must develop a stronger and more secure sense of self. She has to come to terms with what her parents can and cannot be for her and stop asking Phil to supply what they failed to.

In his guide for couples, *Getting the Love You Want,*

marriage therapist Harville Hendrix suggests that our reason for choosing the partners we do is that we want to be safe, healed and whole. He thinks the key to achieving this is to move from an unconscious to a conscious marriage. In other words, we name the goals we were only dimly aware of in choosing a partner and make them the conscious basis for psychological and spiritual choices in marriage.

Among the suggestions Hendrix makes for doing this are several which apply to the point we are discussing. First, we need to create a more accurate image of our partner. When we marry we often think of our mate as someone who will save us and make us whole. We confuse them with our parents or primary caretakers. Gradually, over the months and years of marriage, we need to see our partner not as our savior, but as another wounded human being who is struggling to be healed. Instead of demanding that our partner make us whole, we learn to look within ourselves for the strengths and abilities we lack. We begin to see that the way to reaching the oneness we desire is to develop the hidden qualities within ourselves.

Marilyn, a prominent attorney, is beginning to realize this after eight years of marriage. She is quiet, industrious, responsible. Her husband moves from job to job because he cannot discipline himself enough to follow through on assigned tasks. He plans vacations on the spur of the moment, and is often humorous and creative. As a way of working on her marriage, Marilyn is no longer expecting her spouse to function for her fun-loving side. She is learning to play herself, to find within herself what she first saw in her husband. Her spouse's challenge now is to develop his own responsible side.

3. Take care of your own unfinished business with your family. Often the interference in our marriages stems not only from past family influences, but from present issues that we are working out in the marriage rather than settling directly with the family members involved. Then the best way to help our marriage may be to deal with unresolved issues with parents, brothers, or sisters. As Harriet Lerner stresses in *The Dance of Intimacy*, our ability to be clear with our first family about who we are, what we believe, and where we stand on important issues, influences the level of emotional maturity we bring to other close relationships. When we can acknowledge and respect differences and yet be ourselves in our own families, we are better able to manage the challenges of closeness and separateness in our other intimate relationships.

This kind of resolution is not the result of fighting and blaming, or cutting ourselves off from our families through silence and distance. It is the slow work of reconciliation that the gospels call us to, the difficult path of seeking more honest and loving ways of connecting with family members. It often means addressing the real issues, following the admonition in the letter to the Ephesians that we "speak the truth with love" and be "mutually forgiving" (4:15,32).

If the resolution we need is with family members who have died, our task may be somewhat different. Then we may need to express some of the things we didn't get a chance to say, perhaps in a letter to them that we cannot mail, or in a prayerful conversation. We may need to do some work on the healing of memories, drawing on the many fine books now available to guide this task. When we have had a chance to process these feelings and issues, it may be time for a ritual of letting go and turning them over to God's care.

One helpful way to approach family of origin issues is simply to begin learning more information about our parents' lives, and gathering a history of our family over several generations. We have found that information regarding such things as where and how our parents grew up; the dates of family births, deaths, and marriages; and how our parents remember their own parents, helps us see them and our other relatives as real people. We begin to realize that they have strengths and weaknesses like everyone else, and we can see their lives—and our own—in a larger context.

Spiritually, there is a call to conversion in each of these suggestions for dealing with the influence of our family of origin on our current marriage patterns. Such actions are one way to translate Jesus' words about loving ourselves and others into the everyday realities of our married lives. The gospels show us that Jesus was very concerned about the quality of our close relationships—the prodigal son's reconciliation with his father, Peter's concern for the health of his mother-in-law, Martha and Mary's grief at the loss of their brother. He showed us that God cares as much for these important connections as we do, and that God's grace often appears in surprising ways as we struggle to live out all the relationships in our lives well.

EXERCISE 7: FAMILY OF ORIGIN

The purpose of this exercise is to make the influences of our family of origin more conscious, so that we can better understand our behavior and that of our mate.

Looking over the following items, take some time to recall and make notes for yourself about how it was in your family of origin. Then get together with your mate and compare notes, answering the following questions:

1. How was each of these matters handled in your family of origin?

2. What does each of you want to incorporate from your family tradition? Any adaptations?

3. What does each of you want to reject from your family tradition?

FAMILY LIFE

Affection, touch	Anger, conflict
Sexuality	Extended family
Family fun	Child discipline
Family rules, adages	Family values

ROLE OF MOM, ROLE OF DAD

Household tasks	Earning money
Decision making	Financial management
Social life	Child rearing

Chapter 8

Keeping Expectations Reasonable

───────── ◇ ─────────

We marry for happiness, and there is indeed much happiness to be found in marriage. But we marry filled with illusions too—about our mate, about ourselves, and about what really happens when two struggling human beings decide to put everything together. The story of the prince and the princess who live happily ever after prepares us poorly for the real event of marriage, which is a good deal more complicated than that and may succeed more in transforming us than it does in fulfilling our dreams of happiness.

This is one of the places where God comes into it. "You have made us for yourself, O Lord, and our hearts are restless until they rest in you," St. Augustine says. We are made for God—nothing else will do—and God is not to be had fully in this lifetime. Which means that we live always with a measure of dissatisfaction. We cannot ask our mate to fill that, or rail at him or her when our heart's restlessness persists. When the smallness and fragility of all that is human impresses itself painfully upon us, it really helps to know that our individual life as well as our marriage rest always in a larger context which embraces, supports, and sustains them. A marriage needs a spiritual expanse in which it can breathe.

What then might a couple reasonably expect of the partnership called marriage?

1. It is reasonable to expect that our mate will not meet all our needs, including some important ones. This is not happy news. But accepting it may be freeing. Our hopes for affection and affirmation, for agreement and support, for sexual satisfaction and close companionship may in considerable measure be disappointed. Many who long for a genuinely spiritual friendship fail to find it at home. Individuals who have certain keen interests, whether it be fishing, reading, or the arts, find their mates largely disinterested and have to do alone what they so wish they could do with their spouse.

It is normal. We have to get some of our needs met on our own and in other places. We have to learn to live and let live. And we do well to let our mate go in pursuit of what gives them happiness, even if it costs money, and not take it personally that we are sometimes not included. People are different and have different needs. We can still be good friends—as long as we do not make these differing needs and wants bones of contention.

Some people talk more, some less. Some are more open to new experience, some less. Some people need to spend more, some less. Some are readers; some are not. Some are gregarious and love to socialize; some seem to find the small circle of family quite sufficient. Some like to travel; others don't see the point. Some observe special events with great care; others pay them scant attention. How can two people put all this differentness together? Only by recognizing that it is normal, and there is no way my mate can meet all my needs nor I theirs. We both require larger worlds than we can constitute for each other.

2. It is reasonable to expect that our mate will make mistakes, fail, and sin, and that some of this will not be pleasant. Our mate will drop and break things, crack up the car, bruise our feelings, and go right on. They will make social faux pas, get fat, forget our birthday. They'll drink, smoke, eat chocolates, and enjoy vanity magazines. They will be overanxious, hypersensitive, or insecure. They'll make unreasonable demands, psychoanalyze us, and compare us unfavorably to others. They may have an affair. What are we going to do?

Human love, as we have noted, is always love for a sinner, and it takes fidelity, patience, long-suffering. Fidelity entails much more than sexual monogamy. It means hanging in through the years, being there in bad times as well as good, forgiving and accepting—though it is also fair to chide from time to time, and it may even do some good. But we might as well accept the fact that we are married to a sinner, and that it was our choice. (Actually no other kind of person was available.) We could go out and look again, but we would probably just be trading one set of problems for another. Maybe our marriage is simply very human, and other couples are going through the same things, even those who look much better on the outside. Who doesn't look better on the outside? We all expend some energy on that.

There is one fact which, besides a spiritual perspective, makes it a little more bearable that our mate is so blatantly imperfect. That is that we are, too, and are just as hard to live with sometimes. If you doubt that, ask your mate.

3. It is reasonable to expect that our mate may not be our best friend. Our mate may not be the person we feel closest to, the person we share most deeply with. This is a shame, and is probably not what we expected or wanted.

But it is often enough the case. If our mate *is* our best friend, we can rejoice.

Studies reported in Lillian Rubin's *Intimate Strangers* show that when husbands are asked who their best friend is, they usually name their wife. But when asked the same question, wives frequently name another woman rather than their husband. And there are some very interesting related statistics. Two-thirds of single men cannot name a best friend, whereas three-quarters of single women easily name a best friend, and it is usually a woman. Male friendships are most commonly based on shared activities, whereas female friendships are generally based on shared intimacies. All of this shows that women and men typically experience and express their intimacy needs differently.

But whether men seem to share very much with their wives or not, the fact that they get something vital from the relationship is shown both in the fact that married men are typically healthier than unmarried men, whereas for women the opposite is true; and in the fact that most married men say they would remarry soon if they lost their wife, whereas half of married women say they would not. Statistically, too, widowers who do not remarry die within a few years of their wife's death, whereas unremarried widows typically live on for many years. So although many parents hope for their daughters that a man will marry and "take care of" them, who really takes care of whom?

But if we are not best friends, then why stay together? Actually, there are many reasons. We may get along very well. We may genuinely care about one another and enjoy many things together. We may know that our spouse depends on us very much, and we may find part of our life's meaning in being there for them. We may enjoy many practical advantages in the marriage, and our mate may leave us quite free to get other needs of ours met elsewhere. What would we gain by leaving? And who says our mate must be our best friend?

But what if our best friend is someone of the opposite sex, or someone of the same sex for whom we have sexual feelings? Then our situation is more challenging. Although some people may differ with us on this, we do not think having sexual relationships outside marriage is either long viable or genuinely good for all the persons involved. The religious prohibition here is rooted in the genuine human good. There is something about a sexual relationship that seems of itself to plead for exclusiveness, and when we are not faithful to that we feel painfully divided within ourselves and untrue; and when our mate learns of our having been sexually intimate with another they feel deeply wounded.

But having fairly close relationships outside of marriage with members of the opposite sex is another matter. As long as we do not allow those relationships either to become sexual or to become so dominant as to impair our marriage, they seem both possible and good. They can be very enriching. But those who enjoy these friendships have to be vigilant about the boundaries, and may discover that they have to let some relationships go because they are too highly charged with sexuality.

We ourselves have experienced such relationships as good, and given each other a large measure of freedom to have lunch, take a walk, or do something else of that kind with a friend of the opposite sex. We both value the freedom and trust we thus give each other, as well as the friendships themselves. When we ask ourselves why this is workable for us, we recognize it is because we know at a very deep level that we are number one in each other's lives and that both of us cherish our monogamy as a great value. We both want to live in a world that is larger than our mate, and we want our mate to enjoy the same scope. We have discovered that men and women can be friends and enjoy considerable emotional intimacy without falling in love or getting sexually involved—if that is what they clearly choose.

4. It is a reasonable expectation that our marriage will be in crisis from time to time. By crisis here, we mean a tough spell, a spell so difficult that we might even think of ending the marriage. Some of these hard times are predictable: the initial adjustments to a married way of life, the challenge of the first child, changes in career, mid-life crisis, the end of the childraising years, retirement, the problems of aging in the later years. Some of these hard times are unpredictable: job loss, sickness or injury, a particularly challenging child, a crisis of addiction, economic recession or depression, an affair, the loss of a child, a lengthy bout with depression, either of us finding more of our *self* and needing to make some significant changes. We treat many of these crises more in detail in the chapters on "Weathering Life's Tragedies," "Surviving an Affair," and "Adapting to the Stages of Marriage." The present point is that with so many possible crises to choose from, we will surely have a few. And this, too, is normal. Marriages grow through such hard times, or have a chance to. People who bail out when the going gets tough miss the opportunity to grow into greater depth and love in the relationship.

In sum, our marriages have a much better chance of being happy if we do not expect too much of them. If we can refrain from asking our spouse to be God for us, or to be the perfect mate for us, or to take responsibility for our happiness, we will probably both live longer and enjoy each other much more.

EXERCISE 8: TRANSFORMING EXPECTATIONS INTO PREFERENCES

In *Lifemates,* Harold Bloomfield and Sirah Vetesse suggest a process for converting some of the demands and expectations we carry into our relationship into preferences. They define an expectation as something you need from your mate in order to feel happy, secure, and whole. In contrast, a preference is something you want from your partner but don't need so desperately that your happiness or well-being depend on it.

1. Identify your expectations. See which of these common expectations you bring to your relationship.

"If you love me you will . . ."

Like my friends and want to socialize with
   them.
Include me in all your activities.
Do what I tell you.
Want the same things I want.
Never do anything that upsets me.
Be on time; never be late.
Never interrupt me or walk away when I am
speaking.
Lose weight and stay in shape.
Agree with me.
Be more affectionate and attentive.
When we argue, be the first to make up.

Stop being friends with people I don't care for.
Make sacrifices for my parents and family.

2. Ask yourself some questions about your expectations. Review the statements you have checked and consider the following questions:

> How realistic are your expectations?
>
> What is it that you are looking for from your partner?
>
> What could you do to create more of what you want and impose fewer expectations on your partner?
>
> Why are these expectations important to you?
>
> Why might these expectations not be important to your partner?
>
> What additional expectations do you have that are not on the list? A useful stimulus is to say, "If you love me you will. . . ." or "I expect you to. . . ." and then write down whatever might follow.

3. Change your expectations to preferences. Take those expectations you consider realistic and appropriate, and express them as preferences, e.g., "I would prefer it if you would. . . ." (lose weight and stay in shape, be more affectionate). Remember it is easier to respond with enthusiasm to a request rather than a demand.

This exercise is done by each partner individually. You can then share the results with one another, or simply let them influence the way you relate. It is important to remember, as we noted earlier, that some expectations are appropriate. If your partner abuses alcohol or drugs, has a history of infidelity, or is abusive toward you, you need to take other action.

Chapter 9

Working on Personal Growth

◇

So often a spouse unknowingly reopens a wound that we have long carried and buried. When Joe looks at other women, Nancy is jealous and resentful. Joe does not know that she learned in grade and high school to regard women as rivals and enemies, that she has never had a strong friendship with a woman, and that she fears she is not as beautiful or smart as other women. Both Joe and Nancy are puzzled by the strength of Nancy's emotions. Assurances of love on Joe's part do not seem to help at all.

Jennifer and Pete argue repeatedly over her failure to return home at a promised time. She cannot understand why he makes such a big deal out of it. He wonders whether he can really trust her, and only gradually begins to connect these scenes with the many times he waited and waited for his dad who had promised to take him to a baseball game or a movie. He does not at first know that Jennifer's action touches his pain at hearing his dad stumble drunkenly through the front door long after Pete had given up on the promise and gone to bed. He just knows that he feels fear and confusion when Jennifer is late.

When we experience the pain of these situations, our first response is often to blame our partner for causing it. When we marry, we hope our partner will make us feel good regarding ourselves, and happy. They cannot. We must face our own problems. Many of us carry the emotional scars of childhood with us into our adult relationships. Fidelity to our marriage promises includes a willingness to look at our own need for personal growth and attend to it.

Psychologist Harriet Lerner remarks in her book, *The Dance of Intimacy*, that she has yet to see a relationship improve unless at least one individual can give up their negative focus on the other and put that same energy into his or her own life. When our energy is directed toward changing a partner or taking responsibility for the happiness of a mate, we are engaged in a fruitless and frustrating task. As a familiar saying tells us:

> After a while you learn the subtle difference between holding a hand and chaining a soul.
>
> And you learn that love doesn't mean leaning and company doesn't mean security.
>
> And you begin to accept your defeats with eyes open and head held high, with the grace of an adult and the grief of a child.
>
> . . . .
>
> So you plant your own garden and decorate your own soul, and stop waiting for someone to bring you flowers.
>
> And you learn that you really can endure—that you really are strong and you really have worth.

Such an attitude enables us to enjoy others as they are, to be intimate in freedom, and to love in an other-directed way.

Paradoxically, this work on self is the best way to improve a relationship. It focuses attention on the one person we can change. It allows our spouse to be themselves and develop their abilities and happiness without excessive worry about us. We let go of stuck patterns and create a new marital dance. We develop a climate of trust within which both of us can move toward healing. Marriage can fulfill our longing to be happy and whole, but it does not happen easily, without defining what we want, or without reciprocity.

In this chapter we want to suggest some guidelines for this process of personal growth.

1. An essential part of healing is naming the wound. Healing often begins when we can articulate our own problems. This is not easy. Many of us grew up in families whose key rules were: Don't feel. Don't talk. Don't trust. We learned that it is not safe to share feelings because we cannot trust that they will be validated by others. Left alone with our fear, worry, guilt, anger and loneliness, we learned that it was better not to feel. So we simply denied these feelings, and became increasingly cut off from ourselves. Whatever our background, most of us suffer in varying degrees from the pain of this loss of ourselves, and we have developed numerous survival skills to cope with the pain.

If in our homes it was not all right to talk about the real issues, things that would upset the family, we denied that there were problems. If confidence, reliability, and faithfulness were not present in our homes, we learned that it was best not to trust that others will be there for us emotionally or even physically. We somehow got the message that we were not good enough, not lovable, or of less worth than others. Along the way, we lost our real self and became more and more defined by the roles prescribed by culture, church, or the needs of others.

The process of healing is the journey back to our true self. We feel emotions once unfelt because they were forbidden or painful. When we are sad or angry, joyful or playful, we acknowledge these feelings as our own, without shame or blame. We learn to express them in direct and immediate ways, ways that are respectful of ourselves and others, instead of disguising or hiding them. For if we numb our pain, we unwittingly numb our joy as well. The recovery of the full range of our emotional life takes time and is not always easy, but it is the path to wholeness and freedom.

Another first step in personal growth is finding the courage to name areas where we need to grow. This includes insight into the past and present circumstances that contribute to our difficulties. We may have lost a parent at an early age, and have a strong fear of abandonment. Perhaps we were the one in our family who always took care of others' needs, and we now feel guilty and selfish if we do things we enjoy. These insights alert us to patterns that need changing in our present relationships.

Naming our pain is not an excuse to blame others, to refuse to grow up, to stay stuck in resentment or helplessness, or to evade responsibility for our own lives. It is, rather, an opportunity to recognize that we are not yet the person we were created to be. This naming includes the conviction that, with the help of God and others who love us, we can come closer to the happiness God wants for us. One of our core faith-convictions is that there *is* resurrection from the dead.

2. A healthy marriage relationship is based on each person's having a strong sense of self. Personal growth does not come as a result of self-hate. Rather, it results from appreciating and accepting ourselves. We can then use our energy to nurture ourselves by saying no to self-destructive habits such as overworking, overeating, starving ourselves, drug dependence, alcoholism, or constant self-criticism. To do this we have to make peace with our imperfections, the sides of ourselves we don't want anyone to know about. We need to turn our self-punishing tendencies into self-affirming thoughts and behaviors. Once we catch on to our negative patterns of thinking, we stop them when we become aware they are going on. We substitute positive belief statements for the negative ones, saying to ourselves many times during the day: "I am good. I am lovable. My life is worthwhile. I can be as happy as anyone."

Books on recovery and healing describe this core self as the "inner child," or "the child within." These terms are used in different ways to refer both to the reality of inner woundedness and to the recovery of our embodied, playful and creative selves. One of the obstacles to this recovery is codependency. Though it manifests itself in different ways, codependency is basically a loss of self-definition. We lose contact with our own feelings, body, needs, power and freedom and live a life defined by someone else. We are anxious about revealing our true self because we fear the loss of others' love.

In *Facing Codependence*, Pia Mellody and her coauthors organize the causes, structure, and consequences of codependence around five "core symptoms": a) difficulty experiencing appropriate levels of self-esteem; b) difficulty setting functional boundaries; c) difficulty owning one's own reality; d) difficulty acknowledging and meeting one's own needs and wants; and e) difficulty experiencing and expressing one's reality moderately. All of these symptoms are manifestations of the loss of our true self and the adoption of a false self or mask for facing the world.

How do we recover our true self? People come into our lives who do esteem and love us, and they offer us a basis for believing more in ourselves and liking ourselves. But we ourselves have a crucial role to play in the healing process. We have to hear and believe the affirming and loving things others say to us, otherwise they make absolutely no difference. We are made happy, not by the amount of love we are given, but by the amount of love we allow ourselves to receive.

In the end, we have to give love to ourselves. The love of others can only prepare us for this and support it. A great day dawns in life when we can say: "I like myself. I am worthwhile. I have good things to share with others." Once that happens, it does not matter so much whether others understand and approve everything we do or not. The ultimate basis on which we can affirm ourselves and feel good about ourselves is that God made each of us and saw that we were good.

3. It may be necessary to seek help and support. Throughout the growth process, we need friends, family members, or spiritual companions to keep us honest and courageous. Sometimes healing proceeds better and more quickly with professional help. In addition to the possibility of individual work with a therapist, there are also many support groups for women and men, for adult children of alcoholics, adult survivors of sexual abuse, and people with addictions.

4. Personal growth is God's work as well as our own. Healing comes not only from insight into past hurts. It presupposes openness to God's gift of wholeness, the realization that we are not our own saviors, recognition that it is God who saves. In her book

GodDependency, Lynne Bundesen reminds us of the biblical message that our lives do not have to be determined by the legacy of the past; each of us can be healed and defined by our relationship with God.

There are many points in the healing process when we are called to let go and allow God to break through to heal us. Some of the most moving stories in the gospels are the accounts of Jesus' healings. Countless persons come to him who are wounded in some way, and he calls them to wholeness. Ultimately, it is God who gives healing, often through others, sometimes quite by surprise.

In *Healing the Eight Stages of Life,* Dennis and Matthew Linn and Sheila Fabricant describe one way to get untrapped from the negative effects of past hurts and turn those hurts into gifts for loving. Because our past is always present not only to us but also to Jesus, we can bring Jesus' love into a hurtful memory. We return in imagination to the scene of the painful event, and then invite Jesus into this memory, asking him to heal us as he has healed so many others. In the visualization we hear his healing words and experience his healing action. This is an exercise of faith in the power of Jesus' love to transform the past, and it is remarkable in its potency.

Becoming whole does not happen all at once; it is a lifetime task that we undertake one day at a time. Healing will always be partial in this life, finding its fullness only in risen life.

Marriage is a graced and growthful way of life because spouses provide one another with the context of faithful love that makes the work of healing possible. Within the setting of such love we find the courage to come to terms with our own inner furies; to mourn our losses; and to let go of hurts, mistakes, resentments, shame, and guilt. Freed from these shackles, we are able to enjoy both personal integrity and the gifts of a deep and intimate relationship.

EXERCISE 9: INDIVIDUAL AND COUPLE ASSESSMENT

These questions are meant to help you identify personal issues that are affecting your relationship. Reflect on them separately and then come together to share.

1. What do I feel grateful and happy about in our marriage?

2. Where am I experiencing feelings or thoughts of uneasiness, concern, anger? What are the arguments and disagreements that recur in our relationship? What do I think are the real issues underlying these exchanges?

3. What am I doing that contributes to any feelings of discontent or unhappiness I experience? As I reflect on our disagreements, what do I feel called to let go of or change in myself that would make a change in our relationship? What steps will I take to begin this process? What do I want to ask of my spouse in this area?

Chapter 10

Dealing with Male/Female Issues

⸺ ◇ ⸺

What does it mean to be a woman or a man in our culture? This question is being examined on many fronts today—from comic strips and talk shows to serious research. The discussion is having a profound effect on the way we see ourselves and relate to one another. Many believe that it is one of the major revolutions of our time.

The question is not simply a cultural one. It has to do as well with the biblical images of male and female, husband and wife. Recent research has questioned the way the Genesis story of Adam and Eve has been used to defend woman's subordinate position and to determine her role in the marriage relationship. Reading the Genesis accounts today, scripture scholars can see that it was not the writer's intention to place woman in a subordinate position. In fact, there is a growing consensus among scholars that a relationship of dominance and inequality between man and woman enters the world only *through sin*. Both male and female are created in God's image, and together they constitute humanity in its fullness.

A more accurate translation of the Hebrew portrays woman not as man's "helpmate," but as a "companion" equal to him. This theme is reinforced in another book of the Bible, the Song of Songs. Set in a garden, the book depicts paradise recovered, and celebrates human love. It is a mutual love, in which both man and woman give and receive, initiate and follow, delighting in one another's beauty. This love, they declare, is "strong as death. . . . No flood can quench it" (8:6–7).

The New Testament also shows us that commitment to Christ demands a new pattern of male/female relationships. Holding up such a vision to the Christians in Galatia, Paul quotes part of an early baptismal formula to show what kind of relationships should exist among those who have joined the Christian community.

> All baptized in Christ, you have all clothed yourselves in Christ, and there are no more distinctions between Jew and Greek, slave and free, male and female, but all of you are one in Christ Jesus (Gal 3:27–28).

The Christian vision calls for a change in ways of relating. Those who belong to Christ are equal. They are not to set up categories of superiority, dominance and control. So, marriage in Christ must reflect this new pattern of relationships between woman and man. It requires mutual respect and recognition of gifts.

The question for most married couples is a practical one. How can we live out this biblical vision in the daily interactions of our marriages? In Chapter 13 we talk more about role relationships in marriage as they enter into a couple's attempts to balance family and work. Here we focus on two other areas where many married couples are searching for solutions to the dilemmas they experience. Our purpose is to invite you to look at these questions in your own marriage. The way they appear may be the same or different from the examples we present.

1. Communication Styles

The most common complaint of women in marriage is that their husbands do not share their feelings with them. And women usually add that their husbands are not really interested in *their* feelings either. For women, this adds up to a deep unmet need for communication. Husbands typically become exasperated in this discussion. "I don't know what she's talking about," they'll say. "I share everything, but she's never satisfied." Or, "I'm just not a very emotional person. That's just the way I am." For men, too, this impasse becomes a pain in the relationship, because it means they cannot meet their wife's needs.

A large part of the communication problem is that women and men often speak different languages. Though there are, of course, exceptions, she is frequently more skilled in the language of feeling, of philosophy of life, of spirituality. He typically speaks the language of reason, of problem-solving and practicality. Neither fully understands the other's language nor feels particularly sympathetic with it. When they talk, neither feels really heard. They break off in frustration. Each is very good at something the other is not very good at.

At the root of this problem seems to be the way we were socialized as women and men. Men start as boys, and a terrible thing happens to a boy when, at age 4 or 5, someone tells him that boys don't cry, that he must stop that or he cannot be a man. Now why do we cry in the first place? Usually because we are hurt, or frustrated, or sad, or needy, or scared. Sometimes we cry also when we are touched by love, or when we are very happy, or when we are angry. When we tell a little boy that boys don't cry, we are telling him that his sadness, his need, his hurt, his fear must no longer show, that they are not acceptable in men. We are effectively *shaming* him for expressing them, indirectly shaming him for even *having* such feelings. That cuts deep.

What is a boy to do? What he does is learn to hide all those feelings he is not supposed to have. He still *is* often hurt, sad, lonely, needy, scared, but outwardly he learns to look as if he is not bothered a bit. Years later, when his wife is trying to get him to share his feelings, she does not realize that she is asking him to reveal what he is ashamed of and has not shared with anybody since he was a little boy. He may know in his head at this point in his life that these are normal and universal human feelings, but he still feels ashamed that he even has them, still more ashamed that someone else should learn of it.

Or his plight might be still worse. He may have hidden his real feelings from the world so long and so effectively that he has lost touch with them himself, and no longer *knows* what he feels—except that somehow he doesn't feel good. If he shows any feeling at all, it will most likely be irritability or anger. He is literally cut off from himself, does not know what emotion is driving him, cannot name what he needs. Fortunately, not all men are like this. But many are.

Do women have communication problems too? Yes, but typically of a different sort. What women are told as little girls is that it is important to be attractive and pleasing to men. Another main message is that good girls take care of others—first dolls, then babies, younger brothers and sisters, eventually anybody who looks as if they need something. Girls are taught to focus not on themselves and their lives but on pleasing and taking care of others. They can feel and express feeling with full freedom—but they cannot ask for very much, because that would be selfish.

Where do years of practice at this regimen leave many a woman as she enters marriage? They leave her with an underdeveloped sense of *self*, along with a strong need to be accepted and approved by others. She feels inhibited against expressing anger because anger is unbecoming to a woman. She feels guilty (selfish) making demands. She feels very responsible for how the marital relationship goes, and so has a sense of personal failure when her husband is not happy with her. No wonder it hits her hard when the marriage proves to be emotionally unsatisfying. But she will probably not express her feeling of betrayal as rage. She will more likely carry it as depression. Again, not all women are like this. But many are.

These are the wounds women and men bring from their childhood conditioning into their adult relationships. Two points emerge. One is that we must be careful not to condition our children to imitate us in our dysfunction. The other is that we must work for our own healing. We can heal. But it is the kind of healing that comes only gradually, by small steps. The first step is awareness, recognizing what needs changing. Then comes the resolution to develop, over time, those competencies that we lack. For men, the task is to go inside and recontact the world of feeling, to start to name emotions, and to have the courage to share them. For women, it is to recontact the deeper layers of the self, discovering what one really wants and what one can do, starting to be more assertive about who one is and what one wants whether other people like it or not, giving up pleasing others and being truer to oneself instead.

Communication goes best between two whole persons, a man who possesses his emotional life and is willing to admit that he is human, and a woman who possesses her self and regards her life as equal in value to his.

2. Sexual Interest

People who meet Sally and Patrick like them immediately. Both are warm and fun-loving, serious about running their small appliance business, yet committed to caring for others. Now in their late 30's, they have been married for nine years, and have a son and daughter. They describe their marriage as a good one, except for a constant tension around sex.

Patrick would like to make love more often. For him, being sexual means being closer. He notices that he feels loved and loving when he and Sally have sex frequently. When that doesn't happen, he gets out of sorts and irritable. But Patrick gets tired of always suggesting they make love, and sometimes just resigns himself to living with less than he'd like.

It's not that Sally doesn't enjoy sex; she does. But she finds that what matters even more to her is the emotional closeness she feels when Patrick really listens to her and takes an interest in the inner world she wants to share with him. She wants the kind of intimacy that comes from talking about their deepest thoughts and feelings. Without that, sex feels empty to her. She can't understand Patrick's ability to enjoy sex even when they have been distant and had no real emotional contact.

Patrick and Sally have talked about these differences, and told one another what they'd like. But it feels to them as though they are up against some deeper issues, ones that don't go away simply with better communication. Are women and men really this different, they wonder?

Although couples are unique in this area as in all others, most must deal with some conflict around the way they view sex and how frequently they enjoy making love. In *Intimate Strangers. Men and Women Together,*

Lillian Rubin examines the basis of these sexual differences. There is no doubt, she says, that male and female sexuality and sexual behavior are shaped by culture. A combination of social norms and our response to them has produced a situation that is common to many couples. For the woman, satisfactory sex must include an emotional connection; this connection must usually precede sex. For the man, sex can more easily be separated from an emotional connection. Some men find that sex opens the way for them to express more of their feelings to their spouse.

This sexual dilemma does not have easy solutions. Solving it will mean changing the way women and men are raised in our culture. Until that happens, what can we do? It helps to be willing to speak one another's language of love. We frequently try to love others the way we would like to be loved. If we feel loved and cared for when someone holds us, or initiates sex, or offers to do the dishes, or listens while we talk about how the day went, that is how we try to reach out in love to others. It is our language of love, so we assume it is the same for our spouse. However, that assumption does not always prove to be true. They may not value such gestures very much at all. We have different languages of love, and one of the challenges of marriage is to learn to speak the language of our mate when we are trying to show them care and affection. What makes *them* feel loved?

As a result of the female and male stereotypes we have been taught to live out, both women and men have lost touch with important aspects of themselves. We bring these partial selves to marriage, hoping that somehow our partner will complete us. But the goal in marriage is not two partial selves propping one another up. Each of us needs and deserves the fullness of our personhood which is stolen from us by false polarizations such as the emotion/reason, connection/distance splits we have described. Men are just as capable of entering into deep emotional relationships as women, and women are just as capable as men of being separate, decisive selves.

Christian growth and conversion call us all to embrace and develop those parts of ourselves we have lost. For many men this may mean a struggle to reclaim and value the emotional, vulnerable, and nurturing parts of their experience. Women may need to befriend their bodies and sexuality, and claim their own sense of self. Marriage keeps the pressure on us to do so, and this is one of the ways in which it is a vocation that leads to holiness.

EXERCISE 10: A DIALOGUE ON GENDER ISSUES

It is often helpful to talk with our mate about the assumptions we have in relation to being male or female. In this way we come to understand how we see the world, how we view intimate relationships, and how we are confined by particular definitions of gender.

Do this exercise in two parts. First, answer the questions for yourself. Then come together to dialogue about what each of you learned.

1. What do you believe it means to be masculine? feminine?
2. Do you believe men should express feelings of sadness? fear? uncertainty? Should they be dependent on others for approval and comfort?
3. Should women feel angry? assertive? competitive? Should they put themselves first?

4. In your own marriage, if you were to show the feelings you don't express because of assumptions about what it means to be male or female (e.g., sadness, fear, anger, assertiveness), how do you think your mate would feel and react?

5. If you changed your ideas about what it means to be a man or woman, how do you think it would affect your relationship?

6. If you have a daughter or son, would you like them to feel differently than you do about masculinity/femininity?

Chapter 11

Deepening Sexual Intimacy

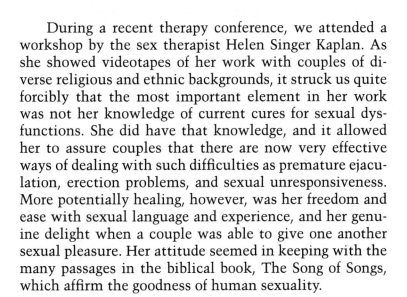

During a recent therapy conference, we attended a workshop by the sex therapist Helen Singer Kaplan. As she showed videotapes of her work with couples of diverse religious and ethnic backgrounds, it struck us quite forcibly that the most important element in her work was not her knowledge of current cures for sexual dysfunctions. She did have that knowledge, and it allowed her to assure couples that there are now very effective ways of dealing with such difficulties as premature ejaculation, erection problems, and sexual unresponsiveness. More potentially healing, however, was her freedom and ease with sexual language and experience, and her genuine delight when a couple was able to give one another sexual pleasure. Her attitude seemed in keeping with the many passages in the biblical book, The Song of Songs, which affirm the goodness of human sexuality.

> Let him kiss me with the kisses of his mouth.
> Your love is more delightful than wine . . .
> I shall praise your love above wine;
> How good it is to love you (Song of Songs 1).

The book portrays two lovers who enjoy one another's presence and affection, finding joy in this gift of God much like the rejoicing we observed in this therapist.

Such rejoicing contrasts with the way most religious traditions have taught us to view sexuality. Sexual pleasure has a bad reputation among Christians. Married couples are now revising these negative traditions regarding sexuality, however, and they are sharing their own experience of the meaning of sexual intimacy. Here are some suggestions, drawn from our interactions with married couples, for developing greater sexual intimacy.

1. Recognize the ways in which your other marriage patterns affect your sexual relationship. Sexual intimacy is one dimension of a marriage. As such, it reflects the tensions and strengths of the total relationship. Most couples realize that it is impossible to be sexually close and loving when negative feelings exist in the nonsexual aspects of their relationship. For that reason, troubled sex is often a signal that we need to work on neglected interpersonal issues—power struggles, fears related to intimacy, blocked communication.

For example, Charles is hurt by the fact that Susan shows no interest in his work and never bothers to ask how things are going. He carries these resentments inside him, making it hard to be loving and warm. Laura is exhausted by the time she works all day, fixes supper, does the dishes, and puts the kids to bed. When Steve, who has been watching T.V. and reading the paper, moves toward sex, she feels resentful and angry. The deepening of sexual intimacy depends on learning ways of healing injuries, moving toward mutual respect and sharing, growing in commitment and fidelity in the total relationship.

Sexual intimacy is also affected by the warmth and sensuality that characterize a marriage generally. Sensuality encompasses more than sex. It is all the ways we make contact and are in touch with one another. It is expressions of affection and appreciation, the support of attentive listening, the language of touch that moves through the day: the warmth of a hug, the gift of a backrub, a walk together in the wind or sunshine, the pleasures of a hike or meal shared. Affection and touch should mean more than that I want sex with you.

2. Keep romance alive in your marriage. Once when we were doing some grief work with a woman about the death of her husband of more than fifty years, the woman shared with us some of the many cards and love letters her husband had written her in the last decades of their marriage.

> "He never stopped telling me what he loved about me," she said, "even though he had already said it many times before. And there were frequent surprises—a rose sent to my office, an invitation to have lunch with him, a balloon bouquet for Valentine's Day. Our love never seemed to burn out."

When desire and passion die in a marriage, it is often because they have not been nurtured. The special things we did in the early years of our marriage get buried by the concerns of work and parenting, or we find it harder to do them in fresh ways and give up. Couples committed to keeping some of this energy alive find that the following ideas help: taking time to be alone together—a lunch or dinner out, a weekend away; planning thoughtful surprises for one another, such as an occasional breakfast in bed; getting a lock for the bedroom door so that privacy is not a problem; taking time to write an occasional love letter or card. Building on these suggestions can help us find avenues for reviving fun, positive feelings, and deeper exchanges in our own marriages. These are the gestures that keep romance alive and give substance to sexual relating.

3. *Learn the art of slow, unhurried love.* Some years ago, sex therapists William Masters and Virginia Johnson developed sexual exercises which they called "sensate focus"— or, more simply, pleasuring. While intended originally to help couples with sexual problems, pleasuring is something that every couple ought to know about; it is the art of slow, unhurried love.

The first approach to this art of sensual loving is through nongenital pleasuring. The couple is asked to find a time and place when they can be together without interruption. The task is to learn to enjoy touching, stroking, exploring, massaging and fondling all of the contours of each other's bodies. The genitals are not to be touched during this first exercise. It is a time to give and receive a total body caress, to let go of performance goals and anxieties, and to develop trustful feelings.

The second phase is genital pleasuring. This is an exercise in giving genital pleasure to one another without intercourse and with no particular interest in attaining orgasm. The lesson being learned is the joy and eroticism of non-goal-oriented sex. Each partner is to be touched in such a way that they feel safe, tenderly appreciated and cared for. During these exercises in pleasuring, both partners pay attention to what their mate does that feels good and pleasing, and what they dislike, and they share this with one another as helpful information.

Couples can develop their own approaches to pleasuring. It can help to deepen sexual intimacy because pleasuring slows down the process of making love, helps us deal with the negative messages we may have learned about giving and receiving pleasure, takes away all pressure to perform, and improves communication about what is happening sexually between us.

4. Deal with your negative messages about your body and sex. Several kinds of negative messages interfere with sexual intimacy. Since such intimacy involves a deep physical and emotional exchange, it will activate our fears surrounding such issues as body image, privacy, rejection, and independence. Women who have experienced any kind of sexual abuse, as so many women have, will have special issues of healing, often centering around feeling that their bodies and persons are being invaded and they need to regain control in order to be safe.

We may have internalized negative messages about our bodies. The media focus on ideal bodies leaves many women and men self-conscious about their physical appearance. When surgery or weight-changes affect our body image, they may revive or strengthen feelings of bodily shame or rejection. These are frequently projected onto a partner as beliefs that he or she will no longer find us attractive and desirable. As such fears arise, it is helpful to name them and to move with our partners in a process of gradual recognition and healing.

Other negative messages have to do with sex itself, especially sexual pleasure. Religious or family influences may have left us with unhealthy attitudes toward sex. We see it as embarrassing, dirty, repulsive, silly, stressful, or sinful. Our attitude may also be unhealthy in another way, characterized by an overemphasis on sex and less emphasis on our partner as a person or the overall quality of our relationship. Sex in this latter case is unintegrated, driven and distracted.

If these negative attitudes are part of our sexual baggage, our first task is to acknowledge their existence so that we can begin to deal with them. This may involve looking at our sexual history in order to understand where we first heard these messages. It may include the healing of emotions and memories, reading that provides new perspectives and information on sexuality, learning to give ourselves more positive messages about our bodies and sexuality, or group work geared to changing our attitudes and actions.

5. *Bring God and sex together.* When our love generates a new life, we see the child as a gift of God and are grateful. In the creation of a new life, we discern the presence of God. It may be harder to see the other ways in which sexual intimacy is an experience of the grace of the sacrament of marriage. The key is the Incarnation, the heart of Christian faith, which proclaims the truth that God has entered into the physical conditions of our existence, so that grace comes through the physical, the bodily. Spirituality and sexuality are therefore inseparable.

If it is hard for us to put sex and God together, it may help to reflect on how much spiritual healing in marriage comes to us through our bodies. We carry in our bodies ancient memories of shame, hurt, and lack of love that often leave us feeling unlovable at the core. God's grace reaches us in a bodily way when our partners reveal us to ourselves as more beautiful than we think we are, when we come deeply into our bodies and experience ourselves as affirmed and loved even with all of our limitations. As we learn in 1 John 4:7–8, God is love.

> My dear people,
> let us love one another
> since love comes from God
> and everyone who loves is begotten by God
> and knows God.

Our experiences of wonder, pleasure, and joy are contact with God's goodness. Touch speaks to levels of the self that words cannot reach, and provides emotional and physical assurance. Its repetition gradually heals at ever-deeper levels. We are loved, and called to love in return. Through such love we experience the sustaining and challenging love of God.

Perhaps bringing God and sex together in marriage means acknowledging that God is not obsessed, as we are, with work and obligation. God rejoices in relaxation, in time for being and enjoyment, in moments of mutual pleasure and bodily wholeness. This is one of the themes the biblical scholar Phyllis Trible develops in *God and the Rhetoric of Sexuality,* as she compares the story of the creation and fall in Genesis with the Song of Songs. Genesis 2–3 is a love story that has gone awry. Joy in the garden ends in the sorrow of exile. The Song of Songs redeems this tragedy, extols the creation of sexuality, and invites us to enter a garden where man and woman treat one another with reciprocal tenderness and respect. They neither flee from nor exploit sex, but embrace and enjoy it. This love is then truly bone of bone and flesh of flesh. Testifying to the goodness of creation, it exists in the context of God's grace.

EXERCISE 11: CARING BEHAVIORS

In our marriage workshops we have asked couples to do an exercise in which each partner writes out for the other a list of things their partner could do that would make them feel loved. When the partner receives the list, they choose three items that they will commit themselves to doing during the following week, without telling their spouse what they have chosen. The items elicited by this exercise usually cover a wide range:

> Walk the dog,
> Give me a backrub.
> Listen without interrupting when I talk.
> Notice what I'm wearing.
> Greet me with a hug and kiss in the morning.
> Tell me you love me.
> Suggest that we go out for an evening of dinner and dancing.
> Join me in doing home projects and chores without my asking.
> Change the oil in the car.
> Call me during the day.

Here are some tips for the effective selection of caring behaviors:

1. They must be specific.
2. They must be positive.
3. They preferably should be "small" behaviors that do not entail great cost.
4. They must not have been the subject of recent sharp conflict.
5. They must not become a list of "expectations" for the other, but rather a resource list each person can use on their own to show the other they care.

Chapter 12

Growing Together While Parenting

———— ◇ ————

Couples who move from partnership to parenting recount a multitude of different experiences, but one thing they all agree on: When the kids come, everything changes. What they mean by everything is their own relationship, their social life, their work, their recreation, their priorities, and their feelings about themselves.

"We were married five years before we had children," Tony recounted. "Now we have four. Before the kids came, we were really married singles, each of us immersed in our careers. We dated one another occasionally. The kids have pulled us together. They have also forced us to decide what our priorities are. Most of the changes we have made in our lives have been for the better. Now she works four days a week and I work three, and we share the parenting about equally. Actually, I'm home with the kids more than she is."

The time the couple used to have for one another is now sharply curtailed. Their time together becomes time together with children—at dinner, in the TV room, even in bed! The nights are no longer their own, even the wee hours, when one or other of them has to get up to tend a crying child. The toll which round-the-clock care takes produces a fatigue which makes sex much less appealing, and sometimes produces general irritability besides. When they would like to slip away to get some relief and enjoy again some of the activities of the past, they realize that money is in shorter supply, and the amount of work it takes just to get everything in order for the kids first and to line up a babysitter makes them wonder if it is worth the effort.

Then there are the challenges of parenting itself. Husbands and wives deeply doubt their own adequacy sometimes as children present peculiar problems: crying that just won't stop, bonding difficulties, a child's preference for one parent over the other, hyperactivity, serious sickness, stubborn resistance, retarded development. Sometimes differing parenting styles, rooted in families of origin, become another source of conflict between the fledgling parents: the strictness of one versus the relative leniency of the other, or the anxious watchfulness of one versus the more carefree looseness of the other. Each is forced to self-examination, prodded toward compromise, pressed to find deeper resources to cope with all these new challenges.

Yet parents seem by and large to love their new vocation, and stretch eagerly to meet its demands. It is exciting for them to see something of themselves in their offspring, to be so totally depended upon, to experience the freshness and openness of childhood, to watch their children's development from stage to stage. It gives their lives new meaning and purpose.

> "I can't begin to tell you how much my little ones are always teaching me about life," relates Michelle. "The things they say are profound.

They knock me out sometimes; other times they make me laugh. What a freshness!

"Every morning my little boy gets up and comes out of his room as if to say, 'It's another day, Mom. Let's go.' "

We have talked with many couples about what develops when they decide to welcome children into their lives. Here are some of the ideas they would like to share with you.

1. Children are a gift and a revelation of God. Sometimes that realization begins at the moment of birth itself.

"Childbirth was a religious experience for me," Therese said. "It was just incredible. Here was this beautiful child, coming miraculously out of my own body, a gift and a responsibility. I could feel God right in the room, and it was as if he was saying, 'Here, Therese and Jack, this is for you.' "

When we get into the work of parenting, we can lose this contemplative dimension, and with it our wonder, and with that the joy parenting offers.

"Sometimes I get so caught up managing the kids and teaching them," Paul said, "that I forget to balance that with just accepting and enjoying them as they are right now. When I do make that mental shift, I really find them interesting. Reading them books, going to the Science Center and the zoo, meeting other families through school—

these are all new experiences, and they're fun.
But probably the most exciting thing of all is just
watching the kids develop."

Children can call forth our shadow side, too, our
darker self. They can remind us of things we do not like
about ourselves, and then we become rejecting and shame
the children. They can bring out our anger, our smallness,
even our violence. They can hook our pride, our perfection-
ism, our need to control. When they call these aspects of
us out into the open, we are confronted once again with a
call from God to a change of heart.

"When we began having children," John related,
"I found myself for the first time understanding
God's unconditional love. I realized that was
how I was supposed to love my children, that I
was the channel of God's own love. To me that
meant acceptance, forgiveness, giving without
asking a return. What a challenge! I believe my
children have shown me the capacity I have to
love *others* unconditionally as well. My wife has
gotten some of the spillover. I'm not sure I
would even have thought of all this if we hadn't
had children."

"Our first child was easy," Mary recounted. "But
our second suffered from attention deficit disor-
der, and it was so difficult bonding with her or
getting anything at all back from her that I began
falling apart. That's when we saw that we both
needed professional help in dealing with her, and
I needed some therapy personally to work on
some of my own issues. Both have been ex-

tremely helpful. I've worked through some old stuff personally, and the situation has become much more manageable for both of us."

It is in circumstances like these that we parents can learn the meaning of grace in our own regard—not just that God loves our children unconditionally, but that God loves *us*, too, just as we are, even when our faults are staring us in the face. We do not seem to be earning love and do not feel worthy of it, yet that love is always there, because God is gracious, compassionate, and faithful.

2. Hang in there through the exhausting times; things get better. Kids move through phases. They suddenly start sleeping through the night. The crying jags come to an end. The extreme shyness evaporates. The child who was so difficult last year mysteriously changes and becomes for the most part quite a delight. Now it's another child who poses the difficulty! Eventually all the kids are in school, and there is a little time for yourself again. A job shift suddenly gives the two of you more opportunity to be together without the kids. The sibling rivalry cools down. The rebellious teenager mellows out a little, and starts to show surprising good sense. It is not exactly that all the problems get solved and stay that way, but that a mysterious power at work deep down in all the members of the family somehow holds it all together, turns despair into hope, solves a problem you were at wit's end with, moves someone in the family, or all of you together, quietly from one place to another.

You too move through phases in the process.

"Our sexual relationship changed with my first childbirth," Joan recounted. "The labor was extremely painful and long-drawn-out. After that, when he approached me sexually, my first feeling was, 'Oh, oh, he can really hurt me!' and instinctively I would shy away. It took me a while to get over that. But I have, and sex is great again. Actually, it's different, better. It has deeper communication in it now, and seems somehow more spiritual."

3. Keep working at time together; but accept the fact that there will not be nearly as much as you would like. Some couples find they have to switch from dinner out to an occasional lunch together. Some find that their much loved weekends away almost entirely disappear, but when they do manage to do it, it's absolutely glorious.

"He changed his work schedule," Sue recounts, "so that two mornings a week we have a couple of hours together after the kids are off to school. We find that's actually a much better time for us than evenings, when the kids need us and then we don't have anything left. We've made an agreement to do no work of any kind during those two hours."

It is paradoxical how the marital relationship can grow even under these difficult circumstances.

"When we got into raising kids, after being several years married without them," Julie said, "I was afraid to ask him how he was. I didn't want to know. I had too much to attend to as it was. Somehow we both just set our personal needs aside and pulled together as a team without saying very much about it. And I think it brought us closer. Maybe it made us appreciate each other more. Maybe we just took better care of one another. Whatever it was, we didn't plan it."

4. *Learn to enjoy one another while you are with the kids.* Being together with the children is, after all, not being apart; it is a new way of being together. And so it is an opportunity to see sides of each other you have never seen before—the nurturing side, the playful side, the resourceful-under-pressure side. You may see less of the romantic side, the athletic, the intellectual, the artistic, because your personal and social lives will have changed quite a bit. Yet you may see *more* of some of these sides, too, because of what the children will call forth. The new sides you see give your relationship more to feed on. You also have different opportunities to show love to one another—love in the form of support, encouragement, and relief.

5. *It's bigger than you are. Put your trust in God.* As parents we generally take our responsibility very seriously. We know there are many adults in therapy working out the damages of their upbringing, and we don't want to see that happen to our children. But what can we do? Beyond a reasonable care, buttressed by some reading and sharing with other parents on good parenting, we can, after all, only be the persons we are. We can only respond to situations as they arise with the resources we have at our disposal. We keep trying to get better at it, but we have to leave the results to God, hoping that God will fill up our deficits and make good our mistakes.

"We had planned to have maybe two kids," Tom said. "We got four! Whatever illusions of control I may have had slipped quietly away. It's often beyond me, beyond both of us. That's where I turn to God, and just keep doing what I can do. Even the financial aspect of it has been a real worry sometimes. What if one of us gets sick, or gets hurt, or the economy really turns down? That too I have to turn over to God."

"When our two older ones started drinking and using drugs," Mickie recalled, "I thought the whole family might break apart. There was constant fighting, and Bill and I couldn't agree on what to do, so we would fight too. It went on for several years. I don't know what I would have done without my faith. I never prayed so hard in all my life. I had to learn to detach, to accept the limits of what I could do, and not to keep blaming myself. Help had to come from someplace else. And then both kids gradually came out of it and put it behind them. Now they're doing just fine." (She crosses her fingers.)

Parenting seems to have its own uncanny power to make each parent grow, to pull us together as couples, and to make our relationship grow. The former ways of relating have to take a back seat for a while to the total absorption of parenting, which entails new ways of relating. It is wonderful when the former ways can be brought forward again on occasions when someone else takes care of the children for a while. But in the meantime, life and love and growth are happening as we stretch to meet the challenges of the new situation, which becomes different again with the arrival of each successive child. It is love that makes the whole enterprise possible, the love that is pulled out of us whether we realize it is happening or not.

"I see life as an incredible journey," said Marie, now raising three small children after ten years of marriage without children. "Our marriage has had two very different phases. The first was enjoying, both of us full of youth and vigor. It was a gift. So is this second phase, though parts of it have been awful. But I don't regret it or want to go back. I feel like the Velveteen Rabbit. My fur has been rubbed off, but I've become more real. I have more capacity to relate to other people now, to understand their problems."

EXERCISE 12: APPRECIATION

One way to grow together while parenting is to recognize the need for, and power of, appreciation in a marriage relationship. Showing consistent and loving gratitude prevents you from taking one another for granted during the stresses of parenting, and it creates positive energy. Attention to appreciation can be especially helpful if you have fallen into the habit of arguing and criticizing each other.

Here are some suggestions for expressing mutual appreciation.

1. Take a few moments at the end of the day to acknowledge each other for all you have done: "Thank you for. . . ." "Something I appreciate about you is. . . ." "The thing I love most about you is. . . ." Don't forget the small or routine things that often go unnoticed.

2. Try showing appreciation in areas where your mate may not feel particularly strong or competent. For example, if your mate, short on confidence as a cook, tries an adventuresome recipe, thank them for it. If your mate is

used to comments about their competency and effi-
ciency, tell them you also appreciate their gentleness and
vulnerability, the way they nurture the children, how
much fun they are at social gatherings.

3. Learn to accept your mate's appreciation and let it
sink in. Don't jump in with immediate rebuttals or deni-
als. Instead, take it in the way parched earth soaks up
water.

Chapter 13

Balancing Family and Work

—————— ◇ ——————

Jim and Sally feel constantly exhausted and stretched beyond their limits. Both work full time. Sally is an elementary school teacher; Jim works for a bank. They have two children who are just about to enter high school. During the week they concentrate on balancing a mixture of demands: meeting the responsibilities of their own jobs; taking their daughters to school, piano lessons, birthday parties, and other events; and spending time with Sally's mother who is a widow living not far from them. By the end of the day, they have little time or energy for talk or lovemaking.

Weekends aren't much better. In addition to juggling family and church events, they try to catch up on those things they couldn't fit into the week, including shopping, meal planning, and housecleaning. Sometimes they wonder if this is how life is meant to be lived. They look forward to a future day when the pace will be slower and there will be time for all that doesn't seem to fit into their lives now. Many things in their own marital relationship get set aside and put on hold as other pressures take first place.

You too may know some of the problems of keeping a marriage alive in the midst of all that life asks of us. Perhaps nowhere are today's shifts in marriage patterns more apparent than in the balancing of love, work, and family. In many marriages, both spouses work outside the home, often due to economic necessity.

But the reasons behind the shift are spiritual as well. Shifting roles have to do with the dignity and personal worth of all members of the family, and with the realization that the home is not simply woman's realm. Research shows that the happiest dual-career couples are those who fully share childrearing and homemaking responsibilities. Husband and children need to learn from caring for a home, and women's gifts are needed in the larger public realm. In the process all become more fully human. Robert Bly shows in *Iron John* that not only women and children, but all the generations of men in a family suffer when fathers are not fully present in the home. This disappearance of the father from the family goes back, Bly believes, to the Industrial Revolution and the change it brought in the working life of men.

But shifting traditional patterns can bring many strains, especially for women, who still carry the major responsibility for housework and child care. This can lead to high stress and result in physical or emotional symptoms. Women end up feeling inadequate in every area, unable to be the kind of professional, wife or mother expected of them. When circumstances require choosing between family and career, it is typically the woman who gives up her job and stays at home.

Whatever the differences in their circumstances, most couples we know find themselves in some kind of juggling act, working toward an elusive balance among the demands of their lives. We've gathered suggestions from them regarding what they've found helpful. Here's what they'd like to tell you.

1. Schedule time alone and time to be together as a couple. This is the number one item on many couples' list of suggestions. The kind of time they set aside differs. Some meet one day a week for lunch. Others plan a weekend away every few months, or a week-long vacation together. One group of couples has an agreement whereby they care for one another's kids on certain weekends. This enables them each to have some time away. Others make arrangements to exchange childcare one evening a week.

> "Planning for this couple-time can get really complex," one husband recently remarked. "It means setting aside some other things. But our marriage wouldn't be the same without it. It not only keeps our friendship growing; it enables us to work together better when we have to make decisions about parenting."

The initial fear many couples have about doing this is that their children will feel left out, that they should be included. A story Madeleine L'Engle tells in *Two-Part Invention*, the account of her forty-year marriage, addresses this concern. Madeleine says that she was speaking to a large library-association meeting when one of the librarians asked her what she and her husband, Hugh, did that was best for their children. She answered spontaneously, "We love each other." She captures the truth that the marital friendship precedes and succeeds both work and having children, and is the core of peace and success in those areas. The greatest gift parents can give children is a strong marriage relationship.

2. Resist conforming to cultural values. Part of the pressure we feel comes from rising lifestyle expectations. Our culture places a high value on achievement and competition. We strain to improve our living standard, to give our kids everything (especially things we never had) to prove we are the best in our professional fields and in our parenting. As Christians, we must ask if this is really the standard we want to live by. What do kids really need for happiness? What do we need? One of our friends refused to buy her son a new computer game for his birthday, in spite of the pressure that all the kids now have one; instead she bought him a parakeet and took him and his friends bowling.

Modern culture raises expectations in us that can make existence a rat race. The demands of life leave us no time to enjoy the results of our hard work. We are always on the run: making it to this or that appointment, driving kids to softball games or play practice, rushing to fit one more thing into our schedules. There is no time to nurture our marriages, to be with our kids, to talk with our friends. Technology, which was to free more time for leisure, has instead made our lives more complicated and frenzied. Our possessions, and the desire for more, preoccupy us. In our frantic effort to hold our lives together, we lose a sense of what life is all about in the first place.

As Christians we need to look at this approach to life and see if it is really in keeping with the gospel vision. We need to ask how our spiritual resources can help us live fully, justly, and generously in these situations. Jesus tells us that the way to happiness is to set our hearts on the reign of God. In the words of an old Shaker hymn:

'Tis a gift to be simple; 'Tis a gift to be free;
'Tis a gift to come down where you ought to
be;

And when we find ourselves in the place just
right,
'Twill be in the valley of love and delight;
When true simplicity is gained,
To bow and to bend we'll not be ashamed.

To turn, turn will be our delight,
Till by turning, turning, we come round right.

By "turning around" we discover the grace and blessings
in our present existence. We see that accepting some limits is the way to finding more life.

3. Foster "family-friendly" work places. If the world of
work were less competitive and more ecologically responsible, it would also be more compatible with marriage
and family life. A new term has been coined to describe
those businesses that are willing to put families first and
corporations second. They are called "family-friendly."
These are working places that provide childcare facilities,
flexible scheduling, pro-rated and part-time positions,
and make it easier for couples to combine career and
family. Much talk goes on in our world about the importance of the family. In reality, however, the family and its
needs are often considered an interference in the high-
powered business world, and in many other fields as well.
The world of work is much in need of redemption.

Changes need to take place in the church as well as
society. One woman expressed her frustration to us. Both
she and her husband work full time, she said. Yet when-
ever the church or school call for volunteers to work on a
bazaar or request cookies for a school event, they call her
and not her husband. When will they begin to see men as
also capable and responsible in these areas, she wonders.

In addition the church has to provide just salaries and
working conditions for its employees.

4. *Make time for fun and play.* We say more about this in
our final chapter. Here we simply want to note that balance in marriage means there is time for laughter, for
celebration, for the spontaneous and unexpected. Otherwise the effort it takes to make things work becomes a
burden that drains the joy from a relationship. In such
moments of leisure we see again some of the qualities we
care about in our partners which get covered over with
concerns and responsibilities: their playfulness, humor,
craziness, and sense of beauty. To get a feeling for how
much difference this makes, try comparing the expressions and exchanges you see in a group of people at play
in a park or at the zoo to those you see in people making
their way to work on a Monday morning. Balance means
allowing space for both.

EXERCISE 13: THE DINNER DATE

Many marriage counselors find that the following
assignment is effective with busy couples they see. Try it
yourselves.

Set aside one evening a week in which you go out for
dinner—just the two of you. The dinner need not be an ex-
pensive one—a hamburger or pizza will do. You are to view
this night out as a regular appointment, a definite commitment, and only postpone or cancel for an extremely important reason. Over dinner, imagine that you are out on a
date, or in the midst of courtship. Thus, you will try to be
as pleasant and as interesting as possible. This is not the
place for quarreling or discussing problems. It is time for
total gracious presence and mutual enjoyment.

Chapter 14

Sharing Your Faith

◇

In an interview on his seventieth birthday, the eminent theologian Karl Rahner was asked to describe in a nutshell the shape of his theology. Rahner replied that his basic theological conviction is this: Grace is the heart of human existence.

If it is true, as Rahner states, that God dwells graciously at the very center of our lives, then sharing our faith is not mainly a matter of going to church together, important as that might be. Sharing faith is primarily responding to the grace that comes in the ordinary moments of marriage. This is the mystery of the Word made Flesh, of the divine permeating the human. Much faith-sharing takes place in ways we hardly notice. We offer here a few approaches for deepening this spiritual dimension of marriage.

1. Noticing the Grace in Daily Events

In *"I" Openers: Eighty Parables*, Herbert Brokering tells a parable about listening to the grace in the ordinary. There was once, he says, a church in which the organ broke. When this happened, the congregation opened the windows and began to listen. They heard the clapping of thunder, the transmissions of trucks, the beat of jumping ropes, the swaying of leaves, the rubbing of branches, the drone of the fan, the walking of women, the running of boys, the moving of traffic, and the whistling of wind. Now *every* Sunday the people do this, and they are thinking of not replacing the organ for awhile.

Couples tell us that spiritual closeness sometimes comes at unexpected times; for example, when they are able to get away for a walk or hike. They share the power and beauty of a waterfall, the splendor of a sunset, the variety and intricacy of birds and wildflowers. Creation speaks of God's mystery and care, and they enter into it in a spontaneous way. Or they find the face of God in the courage of a child's first tentative steps, in each other's warm embrace after a long day, in shared laughter around a supper table with friends. The grace in these moments need not, and sometimes cannot, be expressed in words. Experiencing it is enough. A friend of ours put it in a very down-to-earth way in a letter:

> The whole human condition is so bloody broken—and I'm broken too—and one wonders how anything gets done, how any kids are civilized, how any institutions are changed, how any hearts reach out and how anyone takes chances—but it all does happen, albeit not quite the way we expect. All I see are little faint glimmers of light and grace; there aren't any wonderful, brilliant moments. I feel very mired in the stuff of life—juice on the floor, students who want security, and a self whose fondest dream is a quiet house. Yet somehow, in and through it all, God is alive and is love.

Mystery frequently appears as a question rather than an answer. During the evening news we puzzle aloud over the depth of evil and suffering in the world and wonder about the power of redemption and our part in it all. We talk about the purpose of our own lives after the sudden death of a friend or when looking at a possible job change. Discussing books we read leads to deeper reflection on issues of faith. All these are the quiet, daily ways in which faith-sharing becomes a part of marriage.

2. Praying Together

In their book, *Couples Praying: A Special Intimacy,* Gene and Judith Tate O'Brien emphasize that prayer varies with each couple; there are no hard and fast rules. There are common experiences, however, and these can be the starting points for prayer: putting up with differences, praying for someone, fretting about the kids, being discouraged, balancing the budget, planning the future, adjusting dreams, reaching out to others, letting go of adult children, worrying, feeling sick. Prayer that is rooted in these daily occurrences reinforces the conviction that marriage itself is sacramental, that the sacred is found right in the midst of life.

In prayer we reveal who we are and who God is for us. When we come before God as couples in this way, we experience each other more deeply and strengthen our bonds with one another. It helps us become honest, move toward reconciliation, experience conversion.

How can you and your partner start praying together? Take some moments before going to sleep or when waking up in the morning. Rest together in God's presence. Take turns sharing with God whatever is most on your heart and mind. Such prayer might go something like this.

Ben: Well, Lord, here I am. I'm not feeling very strong tonight. It looks like I might lose my job after all, and I have to admit the thought is terrifying to me. Help me somehow find a way to pay the bills and be there for Sue and the kids. I know you're with us, even though I can't feel much comfort right now.

Sue: Dear God, I'm worried about the same things, but what's also hard for me is knowing how to be there for Ben. Show me how to be loving and a support when he seems so down that I can't reach him. Thank you for what we have; don't let us take that for granted, even in this hard time. We want to keep trusting in you.

If it is hard to get started, you might begin with a short scripture passage and talk about what it means to each of you; then address a prayer to God that is evoked by hearing the passage. Lift up one by one the people you both care about, and offer a prayer for each. Try adding a hymn to your prayer if you like to sing. Some couples say that it helps them to hold hands or physically touch one another when they pray. If you are drawn to centering prayer or silent meditation, do this in each other's presence, finding strength in one another's faith.

3. Participating in a Faith Community

Our sharing as a couple needs to be supported and challenged by the larger faith community. Within this community we find strength in difficult times, the friendship of others who care about us and our lives, and new insights into our faith. This community can also become a place where we and our children face key moments—births and deaths, marriages and anniversaries, and all those other special times we want to mark in the presence of those we love. Not only do we receive much from this participation, we have an opportunity to give to others. This deepens our conviction that we go to God together. These communities are also crucial to our efforts to work for justice and peace in the world, a form of faith-sharing that we treat in Chapter 17.

The sacraments we celebrate with a community are meant to highlight and clarify all those sacramental moments that occur throughout our married lives. They prepare us to recognize the presence of God in ordinary events, and the dying and rising that is the pattern of our lives together. Marking the seasons of the liturgical year—Advent, Lent, Easter—with others enables us to enter into various facets of the gift of God and challenges us to keep alive aspects of our spirituality that we might otherwise neglect.

Couples find that becoming a part of regular celebrations of the eucharist, attending adult education programs, making parish retreats, or joining prayer and scripture groups can bring new life to their faith-sharing. Communities also root us in the larger traditions of faith. We come to see our faith as a gift handed down through the generations.

4. Creating Rituals for Special Times

During our marriage enrichment workshops we ask couples to share a simple ritual. They are to face one another and take turns asking forgiveness for having hurt each other in some way. Each then responds, adding some non-verbal gesture to their words. The ritual might go something like this:

> *Jeannie:* "Paul, I realize that I've hurt you by criticizing you often for little things you've done, and by shutting down and closing you out

when I get angry and depressed. I'm sorry, and I ask your forgiveness."

Paul: "Jeannie, I forgive you, as God has forgiven us both."

Paul: "Jeannie, I know I cause you pain when I'm too busy and distracted to listen when you want to talk with me, and by being irritable and sarcastic when I'm tired. I ask you to forgive me for these things and for the other ways I hurt you."

Jeannie: "Paul, I'm happy to forgive you, as God has forgiven us both."

Rituals are ceremonies or symbolic actions which mark special events and transitions. We are familiar with those major rituals of our faith, the sacraments, but we sometimes forget that we need smaller rites to move us through other important moments. They are signs or gestures that express what lies deep in each of our hearts. Without such ritual acts, our loving and longing, failures and successes, fears and joys, misunderstandings and loneliness, remain locked within us.

The rituals we create as a couple can be simple ones: lighting a candle and remembering prayerfully all those people who are special to us; blessing our spouse or our children as they leave on a trip or face a difficult day; returning in a spirit of gratitude and fun to a place important to some stage of our relationship; exchanging cards or gifts on days that mean something to us; fasting, making donations, or offering shared service to those in need during the Lenten season.

In her book, *To Dance With God*, Gertrude Mueller

Nelson provides a wide array of possible family rituals. She suggests, for example, a way of making meal prayers more satisfying. All family members write down their favorite quotations on a card and slip them into a box. These come from psalms, from scripture, from reading done. Members then take turns reading one of these before dinner, their own or one drawn at random from the box.

Creating rituals calls for a certain slowing of our pace. It asks us to become aware of the seasons in our own lives, in nature, in the church year. This can be difficult when our lives are already stressed and full. However, the time we take for ritual rewards us by giving depth, joy, and meaning to the events we are experiencing.

5. Respecting Religious Differences

What we have said so far may seem fine if you and your spouse have similar approaches to faith. If not, it probably appears difficult, if not impossible. In fact, religion is frequently a source of conflict and misunderstanding in marriages. Couples often come from different religious traditions. Or, both may be Christian but have learned to understand their faith in different ways.

Take Sylvia and Dick, for example. Both were raised Catholic, and both attend mass regularly. Beyond that, Dick has very little interest in religion, and he considers personal prayer and spirituality a bit suspect. He has strong ethical convictions, and contributes several hours a week to a food bank, but he doesn't like to talk about his faith, and religious emotion makes him uneasy. Sylvia finds this lack of spiritual sharing a real loss in their marriage. She attends prayer classes, reads theology books, and makes retreats, resenting the fact that Dick is not willing to be more open about his faith.

In this area, as in others, how we handle differences

is crucial. Declaring one way wrong and the other right, working to get the other person to come around to our way of thinking—these simply lead to greater conflict. Other approaches promise a richer dialogue and sharing: respect for another's position and their right to believe as they choose; the kind of listening that enables us to learn from one another and deepens understanding of why we believe the way we do; willingness to explore some aspects of the other's approach; a method for negotiation and decision-making when our differences affect others, e.g., children or extended family.

What we sometimes forget when we become mired in our religious differences is that the most important sharing of faith concerns what we have in common: the grace and mystery at the heart of our relationship. Starting with those moments when the divine reaches us in ordinary human experience prepares a foundation for dealing with the other dimensions of faith in our lives.

EXERCISE 14: PRAYING WITH SCRIPTURE

This is a simple way of using scripture as part of your prayer together; it takes anywhere from fifteen to thirty minutes. Many of the couples we have worked with individually or in groups find that it provides them with some structure as well as spaces for personal prayer.

Take a few moments to become externally and internally quiet, open and receptive to the word of God. Then the same passage of scripture, any passage, is read aloud three times, at intervals.

The following are some suggested passages you might use:

1. *Gratitude:* Psalm 104; Luke 17:11–19; Psalm 116
2. *Suffering:* Mark 14:32–42; Psalm 23; 2 Corinthians 1:3–7
3. *Reconciliation:* 1 John 1:6–10; Ephesians 2:12–16
4. *Accepting Love:* John 15:9–13; Luke 7:36–50; Isaiah 43:2–7
5. *Children:* Matthew 19:13–15; Mark 9:33–37; Luke 10:21–22

After the *first* reading, in the meditative interval that follows, each partner is invited to echo back words and phrases from the text which struck them. There should be brief pauses between these contributions, so they can be absorbed.

After the *second* reading, in the meditative interval that follows, each is invited to state briefly what they hear God saying to them in the passage, e.g., "I hear God calling me to a deeper trust." "I hear God telling me I am loved." Again, there should be pauses between the contributions.

After the *third* reading, in the meditative interval that follows, each is invited to address God directly in brief prayer. Close with a favorite prayer.

Chapter 15

Weathering Life's Tragedies

———— ◇ ————

One Sunday morning several years ago, we were awakened by a phone call telling us that the teenage son of close friends of ours was fighting for his life in a local hospital. He and a group of friends had been to a party and, on the way home, he had been thrown from a car when the driver lost control on a curve and plunged over an embankment. The boy later died. During the weeks and months that followed, the accident and his death drove a deepening wedge into our friends' marriage. Their grief and pain over his loss became translated into angry arguments and accusations of blame. The wife thought her husband should never have allowed the son to run around with that group of friends in the first place. Her husband accused her of neglecting their son while she concentrated on her job. The arguments gradually grew more heated. Eventually the strain became too much, and they separated.

When we promise to stay together "in good times and in bad," we have little sense of what that will mean over the years of our marriage. We make this promise trusting the strength of our love to carry us through difficult times. The hard times do not always arise from within the relationship. Many forms of tragedy touch our lives as well: the loss of a child through sickness or accident, failure in a

133

business venture, a partner's struggle with chronic physical or mental illness, the sudden death of family members or close friends. Suffering and loss not only challenge individual faith; they stretch the resources of a marriage. That is why couples need to know how to mourn together.

Tragedy can deepen and solidify a relationship. It can also break it. Some couples make it through a traumatic event only to separate shortly afterwards. What are some ways to move through suffering together? All of the skills of marriage that we have developed along the way will be called into service at the time of a tragedy. In addition, there are some specific suggestions we have developed through our work with couples in the midst of such events.

1. Give yourselves space and time to grieve. Grief is a little-understood process. It is really a mixture of emotions—anger, guilt, sadness, reproach, yearning, helplessness, anxiety. These feelings are a healthy and necessary response to the pain of loss. But they feel awful. When a child dies, we may be angry at God, ourselves, the doctor, or our spouse. After an accident, we may agonize over questions of "Why didn't I . . . ?" or "If only we had. . . ."

A health crisis experienced by one partner has an emotional impact on both. When a spouse has a heart attack or is diagnosed with a chronic disease, we may experience a confusion of emotions. At first we may be very frightened. Later we may resent that it came at a bad time or feel that we were somehow responsible, and then have guilt. The sick spouse may feel worthless or inadequate, tense and irritable. Then we feel resentful that we have to put up with this. When such feelings smolder, they are destructive. It is better to bring them out into the open.

Feelings need expression if we are to heal. They may create problems in an intimate relationship, however, unless both spouses understand the grieving process and know that such strong emotions are healthy and normal. We also need to be able to weather their presence. Our society places a premium on self-control, and applauds as courageous those who do not "fall apart." When we feel we must put up a brave front in public and at work, this can put greater pressure on the few relationships where we are free to be ourselves and let our feelings out.

What can help us get through this time? Understanding and patience. The realization that it will not last forever. When we become the object of a mate's anger or accusations—or when we find ourselves directing our own grief at a mate—it is helpful to remember that we are not the enemy. Suffering, tragedy, senseless evil and loss are the enemy, even though our pain in face of these mysteries is turned toward the nearest object at hand. What we really need to do is pull together, supporting one another.

2. Respect one another's different grieving styles. Each person's grief is unique. A husband and wife may vary greatly both in the shape their grief takes, and how long the healing process lasts. These differences in grieving styles are one source of misunderstanding in a marriage. Differences sometimes appear along male/female lines, although not always. One partner may grieve by crying and talking about the event. The other may not cry and may need to do something concrete to express the feelings. One man tells how his father, after their barn burned down, got on his tractor without saying a word, and rode through the fields all night. Because of the social taboos against men's expression of feelings, many men may be unable to cry in face of a loss. A wife may interpret this as lack of caring; the man, in turn, may find it hard to accept or tolerate his wife's intense emotional expression and may seek distance from it.

This respect extends to length of mourning. We frequently tell ourselves we should be over a loss, and are bothered when we still have strong feelings. It complicates things to have a spouse commenting on how fast or slow we seem to be at handling something. Many factors influence the intensity of loss and grief, including our closeness to the person or object, the number of losses we are experiencing at the same time, the suddenness of the loss, and our control or lack of control over it.

3. Draw on outside sources of support. We draw strength as couples from the larger communities of faith and friendship which surround us. This is true especially in times of loss and tragedy. If we try to go it alone, sharing our pain exclusively with one another, it is much harder to bear. So one thing a couple can do is give one another permission to draw on a wider circle of support. These communities may rally to our side at the first news of a death or accident. That is usually not when we need them most. At that point we are often in shock, too numb to feel. Later, when we begin to sense the depth of our loss, friends may have returned to business as usual. It is then that we need to ask for the help we need.

This support can take as simple and necessary a shape as quiet listening. When a loss affects one marriage partner more directly, as with the illness or death of their own family member or friend, it is easier for the other partner to be there for them. But when the tragedy strikes both of us directly, it is not always possible to be present to the other's grief process while attending to one's own. This is when other friends can be of invaluable help just by being there for support. A faith community can also make present the power of God's faithful love and Jesus' dying and rising as we face these critical passages in our lives. A wife who called to ask for our prayers when her husband was diagnosed with terminal cancer said that she needs to know friends and community are there for her when her strength begins to waver. We draw energy and courage from the love of others. We may also need more specialized help in the form of a caring therapist. **4. Develop rituals to assist your healing.** One of the issues a married couple brought to counseling was the wife's resentment over the way her husband had responded to her father's death. She had been very close to her father, and though his death was not unexpected, it was a very hard loss for her. Her husband had been attending a conference at the time of the death, and chose to finish his business rather than return home to be with her for the funeral. Even when he got home, she felt he had little understanding of her loss, and showed minimal interest in the details of the death and funeral. Though time passed, the wife continued to feel the resentment, and it came up repeatedly as a theme in their arguments. This is the assignment they were given which began to heal the resentment the wife felt: They were to visit the cemetery together, and the husband was to buy a bouquet of flowers to place on his father-in-law's grave. As part of the visit, the husband was to listen fully to his wife's account of the death and funeral, and to the depth of her feelings for her father.

Rituals are symbolic actions that help to elicit and guide the grieving process. They give scope for our emotions. Sharing rituals as a couple or a family can help the loss become a strengthening bond rather than a divisive issue in the relationship. Some rituals couples and families have done together include: planting a tree in memory of a person; traveling together to the site of an accident and praying, talking, and crying together in that place; creating a prayer service using favorite scriptural passages in order to remember, mourn, and give thanks.

These are a few suggestions for moving through tragedies as a couple. It is often easier to handle the good times, to feel positive about our partner and our marriage when things are going well. The deepening of our faith and our marriage may come, however, precisely in those times when we must trust most fully in God's love and grace to carry us through difficulties. Though we would never choose to experience these sorrows, when we can manage to support one another during them, we discover deeper dimensions of ourselves, our partner, and our love in the process. We forge a bond that can sustain not only great joy, but deep grief as well.

EXERCISE 15: PLANNING A RITUAL

Rituals and ceremonies take into account our human experiences of loss, grief, sickness, and pain. They slowly help with the transforming of our painful feelings into hope and salvation. If you would like to create a ritual to help you deal with the memory of a past tragedy or with feelings around a present experience of loss, here are some elements you can include.

1. *Readings.* These can be biblical passages that offer you comfort and courage, such as Psalms 40, 42, 43; Isa-

iah 40, 61; Matthew 14:22–33; Luke 12:22–32; 2 Corinthians 4. You may also want to use selections from other inspirational writings.

2. *Prayers.* Simply pray from your heart, or use some favorite prayers or litanies.

3. *Symbols.* Flowers, baskets of fruit, photographs, water, oil, food. Bring into your ritual anything that helps to capture the meaning and depth of the event.

4. *Music.* Hymns or songs you want to join in singing. Quiet instrumental music.

5. *Symbolic actions.* The entire ritual is a symbolic action, but there are also smaller actions that are a part of the whole. Light a candle or several candles. Include blessings. Plant seeds or a tree. Join hands or form a circle. Pour water. Share a meal.

Bring these elements together in any way that expresses the meaning of the event for you and your loved ones.

Chapter 16
Surviving an Affair

— ◇ —

Sexual monogamy proves to be a difficult ideal for many people. In recent surveys, some two-thirds of men and slightly over half of women report having had an affair or at least extramarital sex.

Common as this sort of occurrence seems to be, it is a terrible blow to a marriage when it becomes known. It is a deep wound to the self-esteem of the offended spouse and to the shared sense of the sacredness of the marital relationship. It shatters trust, because now I do not know how you really feel about me, now I do not know what you are up to when you are out of my sight, now I do not know if I can believe your words since you lied to me several times to cover your tracks. All these effects constitute compelling reasons never to have an affair, and, if you feel yourself slipping toward one, to pull back and bear the pain of letting your fantasy go.

Yet many a marriage has survived an affair, though probably as they were going through the rehabilitation process both members of the couple wondered if they *could* survive it. The positive side of the crisis of an affair, as of every crisis, is opportunity. Here the opportunity is for the married couple to examine together the problems of their relationship and to make the changes they need to make.

How Affairs Happen

An affair is a symptom. It incubates always in the context of marital unhappiness unaddressed. Beautiful people are always passing by, and, in a society where mobility is easy and privacy is not hard to get, anyone can have an affair at any time and keep it secret at least for a while. So why aren't we all having affairs? Because when we are basically happy in the relationship we are in, and are mature enough to understand both the limitations of an affair and its costs, we do not dwell very much on the beautiful people passing by. But when we feel lonely and unappreciated, and lack the maturity to know those limitations and those costs, it is very hard *not* to dwell on the beautiful people passing by, especially if one of them smiles at us.

People do not exactly set out to have an affair. It develops gradually, sometimes imperceptibly, out of an existing relationship which carries some erotic energy. At a certain point in the development, the two people realize it is happening, or has happened. *That* is the moment of choice.

Human motivation is usually complex, not all the components of it even conscious. Sometimes it is only after an affair has run its course that a person can name why they did it. They may have done it to hurt their spouse, because *they* felt hurt, usually rejected. Sometimes it is an effort to prove something, both to one's spouse and to oneself: "I'll show you I can be loved in a way you've never loved me." Sometimes it is done precisely to get the spouse's attention where nothing else has worked, to sound the alarm in the hopes of being able somehow to jumpstart a dead marriage. When these motives are at work, the philandering party will at some point become careless about covering the trail, since at some level they *want* to be discovered. Sometimes an affair is a stab at recovering one's lost youth. Sometimes it is driven primarily by a hunger for a more exciting sexual experience or deeper emotional intimacy. Sometimes it is just an attempt to escape the dull routine of married life, a quest for that wonderful initial stage of being madly in love. Often it is several of these things mixed together.

The Process of Recovery

When an affair comes out into the open and the marriage suffers the blow, can the couple recover? They can, but they have to want to, both of them. And they have to give it time. The process of recovery begins with a profound apology from the person who has erred, assurance that he or she has broken off the affair and will have no further contact, and the promise that this kind of behavior will never happen again. Then the couple has to begin talking about their own relationship in a way they have not been talking for some time, no longer avoiding the difficult issues nor attacking one another over them. It is time for the opening up of feelings—of the pain that has festered within, of the needs and wants that have gone unmet. It is a time for listening and for reflecting on oneself. The couple has to face together the shortcomings in their relationship which provided the fertile ground for the affair, and see what they can do about them. Both persons will have to make some changes. Both are called to a change of heart.

The offended party would doubtless find it most comfortable to be the totally innocent one and make the other person the villain. He or she certainly feels plenty of hurt and anger, and the other person cannot deny their guilt. But a deeper look at the situation almost always shows that both parties have contributed significantly to the deterioration of the marriage, and both must change to make the relationship work again.

When Bill had an affair with a woman at work some eight years and two children into his marriage, his wife Mary was devastated. She became obsessed to know the details of the affair—how many times they had had sex, where and when they got together, what Karen had that she didn't have, what Karen gave him sexually that was so special. Bill didn't want to talk about any of it. For one thing he was ashamed and it was a very painful subject for him. For another, everything he had told Mary so far in answer to her incessant questions had just wounded her more deeply. She would take it in and sit with it for days, letting it eat her up, then bring it back and ask more questions about it. This is not an uncommon response, coming partly out of a new insecurity, partly out of a desire to punish by coming back repeatedly to the wrong-doing and rubbing the culprit's face in it. But if the couple is to heal, the energy badly needs refocusing. It really does not do Mary any good to learn more about Karen or the details of the affair. Some things are better left in the shadows. She *does* need to know that Bill has ended the affair and that he really wants to be in this marriage. The energy then needs to go into working on their own issues and giving the wounds time to heal.

What does Bill need? First, he has to make some hard decisions. He has to decide whether he wants his marriage or not. If he does, he has to say goodby to Karen and say it completely: no more meetings, no more letters, no more calls, no more anything. That may seem dire, but it is the only way he can get his heart back into his marriage, and the only way Mary can ever risk giving her heart to him again. So Bill has to die a death and get through his grieving, and he has to let somebody else help Karen die her death and get through her grieving or they will just get reinvolved. He needs understanding as he gets through this painful period, and Mary will probably not be able to give him very much because she hurts too much herself. Besides letting go of Karen, Bill has to re-invest himself in his marriage, a relationship which has been unsatisfying and difficult for him in some ways and is now upended besides. It is a tough assignment.

It would be difficult to name a time when a married couple more needs their spiritual resources than they do when trying to recover from an affair. The whole issue of commitment is reopened for prayerful reflection and choice. The offended party needs God's help to heal from deep pain and to be empowered to forgive and entrust self in love again. The offending party needs God's help in order to let go of someone who has become dear and seems so filled with promise, and to have hope enough to reinvest in the marriage. Both husband and wife need courage to be able to look at the problems in their relationship and make the necessary changes. This is a time for falling back on the God who sustains us when we hardly know how to sustain ourselves.

Because both members of the couple need so much understanding and support during the recovery period, and because it is so difficult for them to bring out the underlying issues and work with these constructively, it is really wise for them to seek professional help as well.

Yet, in working with couples in this painful crisis, we have been amazed again and again at the strength of the marital bond. There are powerful forces that hold married people together, and time does heal. Like many other couples, Bill and Mary moved through their trial and came out of it with a better marriage. Each was able

to take responsibility for their part in the marital dysfunction and to move toward change. For Mary to be able to
trust Bill again and to put the affair behind her, Bill had to
show a record above all suspicion for well over a year,
both in his truthtelling and in his dealings with women.
For Bill to be able to reinvest in his marriage, Mary had to
take his needs in the relationship more seriously and to
let the matter of the affair drop from conversation—even
when she was angry. And Bill had to mature enough to
see that every marriage is imperfect and that an affair is
no solution to its deficiencies.

One final word of advice, grounded in abundant experience. If you have had an affair and your spouse does not
know about it and the affair is over, don't tell your spouse
about it. It hurts too much and will throw your marriage
into terrible turmoil even if the affair happened many
years ago. You undoubtedly love your spouse and you
carry a burden of guilt, or you would not want to tell. But
there is a better way to deal with the matter. Love your
mate in other ways. Really put yourself out for him or
her, and in this way make up for what you have done. If
you need to share your story with someone to get rid of
your guilt, share it with someone other than your spouse.
Tell your pastor. Tell your therapist. Or tell a friend who
can receive it with understanding and forgiveness and
keep it to themselves. But don't tell your mate. There is
no need now, and it will just damage your relationship.

EXERCISE 16: TRUST-BUILDING
COMMUNICATION

The focus of this exercise is on building trust.
Choose a time when you can talk without being inter-

rupted. Then take turns completing the incomplete sentences, following the pattern presented below for listening with care.

1. *The Sentences*
What I like best about my work is . . .
What I like least about my work is . . .
The three specific things I feel most grateful for are . . .
What I am most worried/concerned about this week is . . .
The two greatest personal challenges I am facing in my life at present are . . .
An important change I want to see in myself is . . .
Parts of my body and appearance I feel best about are . . .
Parts of my body and appearance I dislike the most are . . .
   Add further sentences of your own. . . .

2. *The Process*
   a. *Listen to myself,* identifying and accepting my own inner feelings, thoughts, needs, wants.
   b. *Risk disclosing* to my partner what I have identified within myself, beginning with the word "I."
   c. My partner gives full attention and *expresses acceptance* of my communication, asking only for clarification if necessary.

Chapter 17

Caring for the Larger Community

—————— ◇ ——————

We recently attended a wedding during which the groom asked for contributions to the church's program for homeless men. The wedding took place in an historic Lutheran church in one of the older parts of the city where many homeless people live. When the groom announced that a collection would be taken, he was slightly embarrassed and apologetic, stating that he knew it might seem odd, but odd as it was, he and the bride wanted to ask support for this program. Actually, we did not find his request strange; it seemed a welcome insertion of the larger world into the wedding ceremony, which on occasion can seem like a romantic enclave separated from real life. Nor is the request unusual when we consider the deeper meaning of marriage itself. Marriage is a way of living out the gospel message, of being a sacrament of love in our homes, our relationships to people, and our service to those in need.

Reaching out to others may not at first seem like a skill needed for marriage. It is easier to see that it is central to an individual's spirituality. The truth is, it is also essential to a happy marriage. Why is this so?

One way to view marriage is as an exclusive relationship, an island unto itself. Some couples attempt to live this way, only to find that such an isolated relationship suffocates from lack of light and air. They feel bored and empty. If a marriage is to sustain itself and grow over the course of many years, a couple must be drawn, not only to one another, but to larger visions and projects. In this way their lives find meaning and purpose, and they are nourished by those for whom they spend themselves. In a Christian marriage, the love we have for one another is always connected in countless ways to the love we have for others.

Likewise, the hope or despair that pervades our married life is not simply created by our interactions with one another; the light or darkness in our lives is also influenced by the state of our planet. Our hearts may be heavy even though things are going well for us as a family. The source of our sorrow is the threat of war in the world, the torture of innocent people, the hunger and sickness of whole populations. The path into the light then is not through more work on our own marriage relationships, but through greater compassionate action. A familiar Hasidic tale makes this point:

> An old rabbi once asked his pupils how they could tell when the night had ended and the day had begun.
>
> "Could it be," asked one of the students, "when you can see an animal in the distance and tell whether it's a sheep or a dog?"
>
> "No," answered the rabbi.
>
> Another asked, "Is it when you can look at a tree in the distance and tell whether it's a fig tree or a peach tree?"
>
> "No," answered the rabbi.

"Then when is it?" the pupils demanded.

"It is when you can look on the face of any man or woman and see that it is your sister or brother. Because if you cannot see this, it is still night."

We are connected to all of the earth and to all peoples on our planet; our joy and sorrow as a couple is bound up with their well-being.

A few years ago we were asked to develop guidelines for a marriage ceremony that would take into account the theology of marriage as well as its cultural context. Our entire committee believed that the ceremony should contain some public statement of the couple's commitment to the gospel vision for the world. So we had the couple pledge themselves, and asked those present to pledge themselves, to meet their responsibilities to the world. How did they as a married couple plan to live out Jesus' vision of love? This challenge shapes many of the questions we need to ask ourselves over the course of a marriage; our answers will change as circumstances shift.

1. How do we want to shape our lifestyle in light of the gospel? If we do not consider this question deliberately at various points in our marriage, we will probably drift into conformity with cultural values. It is easy to drift when there are so many other things clamoring for attention. We buy more and more things we don't really need. Our standard of happiness becomes the amount of money we are making, the kind of home we own, the vacations we are able to afford. Lifestyle decisions are implicit in many of the things we do in an almost automatic way daily. How many cars will we have? Will we drive to work or use public transportation? What kind of a house do we want, and in what neighborhood? Questions like these keep us centered on Christian values as we make our daily purchases and direct our lives in terms of time and money. If we do with less, we can give more to others, as well as tax the world's resources less. Each couple will answer these questions differently, but part of the challenge is to keep them alive within our marriage, so that we do not fall into patterns without thinking about them.

Many of us are already living with limited resources ourselves, and have little money to spare. There are many ways of reaching out that do not involve money. It may be a matter of sharing our time and talents, of raising awareness, of parenting for peace and justice, of working against violence and racism in our neighborhoods. Our contribution may seem small and insignificant, but as Gandhi reminds us: "Almost everything you do will be insignificant, but it is very important that you do it." Small actions build on other small actions and soon become a powerful force for hope.

2. What will we do about differences in values and commitments? Marge and Steve, a couple married twenty years, have struggled with some value differences. Steve works hard, makes a very good salary, and they live well. Marge has a part-time position in their church, and plans many of the peace and justice projects for the community. They have argued for years over the use of their money. Marge wants to live more simply and give more of their resources to those in need. Steve is willing to share, but believes that he has earned what they have and others could do the same if they were willing to work as hard as he does. He sees no reason why they shouldn't enjoy nice vacations and a beautiful home.

These diverse values have called for much communi-

cation and compromise. Marge and Steve are continuing
to deal with them. Neither is yet completely at peace
with the way they allocate their money, but both have
grown in many areas. They now share more with others
than Steve would initially have done. They have found
ways to become more sensitive to global concerns as they
plan their vacations. Their children have been a part of
many of their conversations and are learning to think and
choose in light of them. In the process they are keeping
alive an awareness of the world's needs and shaping a
commitment to help meet them.

Some couples solve this dilemma by allowing greater
scope for individual differences, for example on the question of what peace and justice organizations they will
support. One couple we know decided that each could
select a cause of special concern, and both would support these selections together. In this case, the woman
wanted some of their time and money to go to shelters
for abused women, and the man felt a commitment to
stopping worldwide systems of torture by supporting
Amnesty International.

**3. What are the ways in which we will keep being con-
verted to Jesus' vision?** Marriage involves a promise to
be grace and challenge for one other. That presupposes
that each of us is growing in our awareness of peace and
justice issues. This can happen in many ways. We can
read and study about the other nations of the world. We
can open our homes to persons of different backgrounds.
We can learn more about the causes of hunger and pov-
erty, and work to change systems. We can share what we
have learned with one another, and bring our concerns to
prayer. Ever we are open to being more fully converted to
Jesus' vision of how the world should be.

Sometimes this question takes on special meaning

when one partner undergoes a rather deep conversion experience. I remember one point in our marriage when Tom was reflecting more intensely on the radical nature of the gospel call after reading Jim Wallis' *The Call to Conversion*. His comments and questions raised a quiet anxiety in me and I felt myself becoming slightly afraid. Though I shared his convictions, I knew that I would be profoundly challenged and affected by the way in which he felt called to live them out. In a marriage, what happens to one partner necessarily has an impact on the other. This question of risk is related to the deeper ways in which a couple is ready to hear God's call and to trust living it out in new ways.

EXERCISE 17: REACHING OUT

List ten things you'd like to do and can do for our world. If you have children, involve your whole family. Make them simple, possible items. Number them in order of importance to you and then begin with number one and work through the list. Here is one couple's list:

1. Share with the rest of the family one newspaper item that focuses on world hunger or raises our understanding of global concerns.
2. Set up a recycling area in our home, and recycle everything we can.
3. Include global concerns, especially hunger and peace issues, in our family prayers.
4. Make a commitment to be informed and vote in every election this year.
5. Drop in to visit the elderly couple who live next door, and see if they need some help.

6. Decide on one hunger program we can support financially and set aside money each month for it that we might have spent on things we don't really need.

7. As a family write one letter of support for hunger or peace-related legislation addressed to members of Congress.

8. Clean out our closets and give unused clothing to a local clothing distribution center in our area.

9. Plan at least one cross-cultural experience for our family, e.g., offer to host an exchange student from another country, invite friends of different racial and ethnic backgrounds to share their experiences with us.

10. Focus the books we choose to read for one month on racism and issues surrounding racism. Share with one another what we learn from our reading.

Chapter 18

Adapting to the Stages of Marriage: I

──────── ◇ ────────

Life does not stand still. It is ever on the move. Marriage is a stable union, but that may be all that is stable about it. It is not the same thing from one day to the next, still less from one year to the next. Each of the individuals in a family is under constant development, and the outer circumstances in which a marriage is embedded are ever shifting too. The only way to survive in a marriage is to keep changing with it. That means being hospitable to surprise and deft at adapting.

While change never stops and tends to be disorderly, there are some predictable major shifts in the course of most marriages which can be roughly charted. Having even a general idea of what to expect can be helpful, giving as it does some opportunity to get ready. In *Creative Marriage*, marital therapist Mel Krantzler explains that inside every marriage there are six marriages, succeeding one another over the years. Each time a couple comes to one of these transitions, they need to rewrite their marriage contract, with new roles and new rules. For if they try to keep living by the old, the relationship breaks down. When couples seek professional help, it is usually in one or other of these passages, because the changes that are required are often difficult and frightening.

We think in terms of seven stages of marriage, which

we will describe in this and the next two chapters, naming some of the tasks of each and the skills and spiritual qualities they call for. The stages are:

1) establishing marital patterns
2) accommodating children into the marriage
3) developing careers
4) facing midlife crisis
5) launching the children and changing focus
6) retiring and finding new purpose
7) coping with aging and dying

Establishing Marital Patterns

The first task is establishing the basic patterns of the relationship. There are many aspects to it: how household chores are distributed, how decisions are made, how money is spent, what sort of sexual relationship is developed, how existing relationships with families and friends are lived out in the new situation, how anger and conflict are handled, how much togetherness and how much separateness there are in the relationship. Couples do not usually consciously plan and lay out policies and procedures in all these areas. But they do inevitably move toward dealing with these matters in certain ways. It is when one or other of them feels the pinch in some arrangement which has evolved that the matter is brought up for explicit consideration. For example, one person is bothered by the way money is being spent, or finds the other's in-laws too much in the picture, or feels there is too little freedom. The irritation finally comes out, and that is when the challenge is faced. So what are the patterns going to be? What agreements can we make that we can both be comfortable with?

It is not just the issues themselves that are taxing. So

is the process by which they are dealt with, for in terms of process, too, the couple is just beginning to find its way. Immediately their capacities for communication and negotiation are tested, and here, too, they begin to establish patterns which will perdure. Do they talk about personal feelings? Do they listen to one another? Can they harness anger? Do they acknowledge their own subjectivity? Can they let go of some expectations? Can they give and take? So daunting are the tasks of this formative stage of marriage that many a relationship ends in the first eighteen months in disillusionment and bitterness. It is harder than it looks. Couples who come for counseling ten or twenty years into their marriage often begin by saying something like:

> "Our problems go right back to the beginning. We never did learn to communicate."

> "We never learned to resolve our conflicts. We just keep having the same arguments over and over again."

> "We never did establish a good sexual relationship. We both knew that, but neither of us would ever talk about it."

Obviously the key skills needed in this foundational stage are communication and negotiation. And the spiritual qualities needed are courage, patience, humility, and large-heartedness. It can be a spiritual crisis. We married for happiness, and we find ourselves facing instead a considerable measure of suffering. We are being challenged to grow in deeply personal ways. The relationship inevitably shifts from the romantic stage, in which we are carried lightly and easily by powerful energies, to a more

realistic stage, in which we must choose to commit ourselves to the challenging business of loving another human being and allowing ourselves to be expanded in the
process.

Accommodating Children into the Marriage

Everything changes when the first child comes. That
is why it is well to have the foundations of the marital
relationship well laid before starting a family.

With the coming of the first child, the familiar rou-
tines of life all change. A third person must now always
be taken into account. The couple is no longer free to
pick up and go the way they used to. Now they have to
get the baby ready and take the baby along—or decide
they cannot go because the event and the baby are poorly
suited to one another and a babysitter cannot be found.
Now the mother, whose main personal interest before
was her husband, is more taken up with the baby and her
husband often feels crowded out. Now there is a whole
additional set of tasks to be done in connection with
childcare, which dominate the days and intrude into the
nights.

Phil and Rosie are a young couple whose marriage
almost broke up in the new situation occasioned by their
first child. Two months after the birth, Rosie resumed
her fulltime work outside the home. She picked the baby
up from childcare on her way home, and was busy with
him through the evening. Then she fell into bed exhausted. Phil watched more and more TV, and the couple
found very little to say to one another. When the weekends came, Rosie, who felt guilty about having the baby
in childcare all week, devoted all her time to playing with
him and the couple stopped going out. Rosie also lost all
interest in sex.

When in counseling we began to uncover all the pained feelings harbored on both sides of the relationship, it became clear that Rosie had built up a lot of resentment against Phil because she felt as if she was carrying the whole burden of the new baby. But if Rosie was feeling abandoned, so was Phil. Rosie was so involved with the baby that she seemed to have no more interest in Phil except to have him do various tasks. She also seemed so possessive of the baby that there was no space for Phil to come in and form a relationship. With Rosie so preoccupied and their sexual relationship gone, what was there left to do at home but watch television?

Getting these feelings out was the beginning of the change. What Rosie most needed from Phil was a complete change in mindset, such that he saw himself as co-parent and co-homemaker all the way. She did not want to have to ask him to do what needed to be done and then see him do it as if it were a favor. She wanted him to take responsibility for recognizing what needed to be done and doing it without being asked. She also wanted him to take more of an interest in the baby, to share time taking care of and playing with him, not just to father by providing—but she needed to learn to make more openings for that. What stood in the way of their former happy sexual relationship was mainly her anger at him but also her general exhaustion. Once they balanced out their new responsibilities more equitably, both problems were greatly mitigated. Phil began positively to enjoy interacting with his little son and watching his development, and found nurturing and caretaking qualities in himself he didn't know he had. Once they got through the crisis of adjustment, the couple found themselves closer to one another than they had been before their child's birth.

As the responsibilities of parenting unfold, and especially as more children are added, the couple take on more and more completely the identity of parents, and their primary focus of energy becomes the family. This is appropriate, but it entails a danger. If the couple are not careful they may fall into neglecting their own relationship, allowing it to be completely eclipsed by their parenting roles.

> "Sometimes I think she is afraid to be just with me," George said. "She always seems to want to do everything with the kids. And you know, I really miss just being with her. Maybe that's why I feel more vulnerable to an affair than I have ever felt before, even though I don't want to do it."

The tasks of this stage, then, are to expand the circle of married love, to coordinate parenting styles and redistribute tasks, and to continue to give time and energy to the marital relationship itself. These are daunting challenges, and again they call on our spiritual resources—thoughtfulness, self-sacrifice, faithfulness, openness to learning and to growth. Many of the years of a marriage are poured into the work of raising children. It is a work of largely unsung devotion, a day-in-day-out dedication to one's responsibilities, a constant flexing with the evolving needs of each member of the family.

It is not all work, of course. Our children make us young over and over, give us many joys, make us proud. That is part of God, too, the gift-giving part. Tom remembers saying to his father, who was dying of cancer at the age of eighty: "Dad, when you were my age you were already a father and sole breadwinner to seven children. I can't even imagine that. What was it like?" His father was quiet a minute. Then he said slowly, with a warm smile, "It was great fun."

Developing Careers

Developing careers is another passage couples typically go through. It is more complicated than it used to be because it is common today for both members of the couple to have careers and because it is not unusual for one or both of them to want to change careers sometime during their married life. These initiatives occasion major adjustments. One member of the couple may have to take on extra work to put the other through school. The family will have less money to spend for a while as wife or husband goes to school or takes a new job with a pay cut in order to gain greater work satisfaction. Spouse and children both have to make sacrifices—in additional chores that need to be done and in the loss of the accustomed availability of parent or spouse. Resentment can build as the full price of making career changes emerges. Anxiety builds, too, as the family wonders what the long-range implications of the shift in roles will be.

Many a woman feels guilty doing less for the family than before, and even asking for family resources, in order to expand and enrich her own life. Her children and husband can *help* her feel guilty—and often do. But this is not a fair response. Aren't women entitled to an interesting and satisfying life, too, and might that not require a larger world than the family, as it does for the man and will eventually for the children? And won't the whole family benefit in the long run from her richer education and experience, her greater happiness, her increased earning power and autonomy?

A close friend has taken a leave from his job and become full-time householder while his wife does her

internship and residency as a physician. They have five
young children, and agreed that one of them should be at
home all the time as primary parent. It was clear which
one that would have to be during this period.

> "It's been quite an adjustment," Jim says. "It's
> harder than my job. There is an immense amount
> of work, which it seems I never quite get done,
> and constant challenges from the kids with their
> many needs. It has really stretched me. But I've
> learned an awful lot, and I know it's changed me
> deep within. It has been a tremendous opportu-
> nity to be there with each of the kids as they grow,
> and that is something I wouldn't exchange for
> anything.
>
> "People's reactions have really been interest-
> ing. Some men are quite threatened by it and
> would like to see me back 'where I belong.' A lot
> of women can't believe I'm actually doing this
> and see me as quite a hero—though some of
> them wonder if a man is really capable of being
> good at this. It's a strange place to be."

A husband sometimes consciously or unconsciously
harbors the fear that his wife, if she ever becomes independent, will leave him; at worst, he fears that that is
indeed her main motive in educating herself and making
moves toward a career outside the home. It *is* sometimes
the motive; a woman finds herself in a very unhappy
situation and realizes she has to develop some economic
viability if she is ever to be able to leave it. But much
more commonly the motive is simply that she wants to
develop her talents, enlarge her world, make a contribution to society.

Still, it can be threatening to a man who has some undeclared expectations about the relationship between the sexes. What if she becomes better educated than I am? What if she earns more than I do? And isn't her working outside the home a negative reflection on my ability to provide for the family? These can be real blows to the male ego. But if a man is willing to reflect and pray about this kind of discomfiture, he might undergo a spiritual transformation and come to recognize the sexism in his assumptions. If he can accept his wife as genuinely his equal and even his superior in some respects, he has moved more fully into the truth, and the truth sets us free. If a man is essentially trying to keep his wife in bondage, and is driven by a need to be superior to her, neither person is very free or whole. If he can let go and support her personal development, he may have to die a death, but both will probably emerge more fully alive, better balanced, and closer friends.

It is true that there is always danger in a long-term relationship that one person will outgrow the other and become bored in the relationship. This may happen through career development, but it can just as easily happen through ongoing education, even if it is only informal, through work on one's psychological and spiritual growth in groups or in individual therapy, or even through regular sharing with close friends who are emotionally, intellectually, and spiritually alive. The best defense against the danger is surely not trying to fence one's mate in, which is neither loving nor fair, but taking care to promote one's own personal development in an ongoing way. One of the best ways to do that is by participating in some of the same activities which are producing such growth in one's partner.

EXERCISE 18: YOUR HOUSE—A FANTASY TOUR

Susan Campbell suggests this exercise in *The Couple's Journey*. It is probably most useful for the earlier stages of marriage, when we are facing power struggles and beginning to deal with differences and conflicts, but these issues often recur at later stages as well. The exercise is meant to help you look at the often unconscious norms about how space is to be used in your house, and to see how this use of external space may be a mirror of your relationship.

Get into a comfortable posture and picture your house as it looks right now, along with any outside grounds which surround it. First, just get an overall view of the house, a general impression. Now, take a fantasy tour of this space. Imagine yourself walking very slowly through it, experiencing whatever feelings come as you do this. Pay particular attention to the questions, "To whom does this space belong? Who controls or uses this space most of the time?" Notice what you feel as you ask and answer these questions. Give yourselves at least five minutes for your fantasy excursion.

The discussion which follows this fantasy tour will most likely lead to a consideration of such issues as: Do we agree or disagree about who controls the various parts of our house? How do we feel about the way things are? Can we see our house as a metaphor for other aspects of our relationship? What have we learned from this activity? Have we discovered any patterns or rules that we would like to change?

Chapter 19

Adapting to the Stages of Marriage: II

———————— ◇ ————————

Facing Midlife Crisis

Midlife crisis is not universal, but it is common enough to merit treatment as one of marriage's typical passages. Midlife crisis is crisis in the sense that it is painful, frightening, and pivotal. It is essentially a period of discontent and self-questioning. It seems to happen around forty, give or take ten years. It arises quite possibly simply out of a sense of the ineluctable passage of time. Among its sentiments are these:

> Here I am, halfway through my life or better, and I'm not satisfied. I'm tired of the work I've been doing, and don't feel very successful. I'm bored with the marriage I'm in. I'm bored with myself. Life is short, and I haven't lived, and the clock runs right on. I don't like the shape my body is in. My youth is gone. I'm trapped. I can't leave my job; I don't know what else I would do. I can't leave my marriage either. I can't afford it. My spouse would be devastated, and the children would never understand it. Spiritually I feel dead, and that feels awful too. I have no direction whatsoever. I keep going through the motions,

but it just isn't working anymore. I've got to do something. But what?

Midlife crisis is anxiety and depression combined, depression about the past and anxiety about the future. The sufferer becomes self-absorbed as he or she goes around and around in self-search. Irritability is high. Negativity and criticism increase. The person might have an affair, just to pump some life back into the bloodstream, to be young again, to feel better about the aching self.

The Chinese character for "crisis" is a compound of two simple characters, the one for "danger" and the one for "opportunity." Midlife crisis is indeed both, its downside danger, its upside opportunity. We need to take seriously this surging systemic need to reevaluate, to get perspective, to make some decisions. That is the opportunity. Here is the chance to reevaluate my life, to decide what it is I really want to be putting my limited time and energies into, and to make the changes I want to make before it is too late. It is also a time for reaching acceptance of the limits of life and of all human achievement, and making peace with myself and the human condition. For that I need God's help. If I shun the soul-searching, find some drug, keep on keeping on, I may well come to the end of my life with a bitter sense of waste and futility.

What does this passage mean to a marriage? It means stress. For the person not involved, it means an exercise in patience and supportive love. Like so many of the things we watch one another go through in marriage, this is an agony we would love to remove but cannot. It is our mate's personal struggle, and they have to sweat it out. But understanding and patient support certainly help.

If we are the person going through the painful soul-searching, it is a call back to our spiritual foundations because it has to do with ultimate meanings and with that unique destiny of ours to which we must be faithful at peril of losing our very self. It is a time to ask help from someone with whom we can sort issues through. That person will probably not be mainly our mate. But there does need to be some serious communication with our mate, both about our relationship and about any other changes we would like to make at this point in our life. It is an opportunity both for readjustment and for deepening.

It should be obvious that the person going through midlife crisis is at spiritual bedrock, and the ramifications of the handling of the crisis are profound for oneself and for others. Carl Jung, the great Swiss psychiatrist, once remarked that he had yet to deal with a client in the second half of life whose problem was not at bottom spiritual.

Launching the Children and Changing Focus

There comes a time, after twenty to thirty years of marriage, when the nest empties out and the parenting years are over. There is some relief in this, but there is also a vacuum. Not only are some much-loved individuals moving out of daily contact, but one's life-purpose of the past few decades evanesces and leaves a void. What is the meaning of our life now?

Because the crisis can be quite sharp, one way parents meet it is by denying it and just continuing to parent. They still busy themselves with their children's lives, call them every day, visit them frequently, enter into their marriages and other personal affairs, offer advice, dispense financial support, conduct rescue operations, and spend much of their own time together talking about the problems of their children. Consciously or unconsciously they want to keep their children in a state of dependency, and thus keep themselves employed as parents.

No one likes to die, and it is not surprising that we resist the death and transfiguration that seem to enter our house just as the kids leave it. After all, our kids are the most important persons in our lives, our own creation and the fruit of a lot of blood, sweat, and tears. These young adults are the extensions of ourselves, our personal immortality. The parenting role has become familiar and comfortable. And the marital relationship without the kids may not contain much promise at this point, may indeed have run dry some years before. No wonder we feel no eagerness to meet this death.

Again the crisis is profoundly spiritual. Does God have any future for me? Do I dare to trust in that? If I do let go, will I lose everything and stand utterly bereft? If I fall, will anyone catch me? It is pretty clear that real love for my kids means letting them go so they can be adults and have their own lives. I have to stop rescuing them and get out of their hair. I know that my solicitous caretaking is now more for me than for them. But if I let them go, I will have to create some kind of new life for myself, and I am not sure I know how to do that at this point. It frightens me, and feels empty of any real value. And if my spouse and I ever stop talking about the kids, what *will* we talk about?

God is always out in front of us, creating our future, and inviting us into it. The specifics are individually tailored, cocreated by God and ourselves, but the call is always to love, whatever that might demand of us. This passage is ultimately about the opportunity to grow spiritually by trusting God, letting go, and moving courageously forward.

And there *is* life after death. To stop parenting our

children is not to lose them, but to begin to relate to them in a different way, adult-to-adult, friend-to-friend. It is a wonderful thing to watch their adulthood emerge, to observe how they cope with the problems of life and how they philosophize about it, to watch them continue to develop as persons through the challenges they grapple with. It is a relief not to have to parent them through all that, but to let them take care of themselves and one another, and just be there as good friends. It is delightful to see them bring forth their own children and grow into the role of parenting, and to know that we don't have to parent these kids but only be loving grandparents, which is a good deal easier. If we have the courage to let our kids be their own persons, we might well end up with a more satisfying relationship with them than we ever had before. Not without loss, of course. They are no longer at home, do not need us as much, and don't call, write, or invite nearly as often as we'd like.

And that leaves us with our marriage and whatever other purposes we might create for our life now. It is time to find new ways to be life-giving and loving, new ways to be creative, new ways to nourish our emotional, intellectual, and spiritual vitality. And it is time for us and our mate to review our marriage contract and write a new one to correspond with the changed situation. What new activities does each of us want to undertake by ourselves? What new activities do we want to undertake together? What are some of the underlying frustrations in our relationship which with courage and gentleness might be addressed now so that our future together might be more satisfying to us both? The call to personal growth and growth together is again before us.

Launching the children, undergoing a midlife crisis, and establishing or changing careers can all occur at around the same time, or any two of them might coincide. Talk about challenge! Life seems to be like that, regularly seeming to overwhelm us, the storm clouds all gathered at once. But there stand all around us people who have survived these things, are still on their feet, and say they are happier in their forties or fifties than they have ever been in their lives.

Retiring and Finding New Purpose

Retirement is the beginning of more time together than we may ever have had before. And if we have worked outside the home for years, it is the beginning of a whole new way of spending our days. This is a stressful adjustment for both members of the couple.

Everything said above about a shift in our life-purpose applies here, and may be felt as even more profoundly disorienting than the end of the parenting task if we have for decades put much of our best energy into an outside job. A feeling of emptiness, of uselessness, is, for a while at least, almost inevitable. So we will probably be difficult to live with at first, the more so if we are also experienced as an intruder into a physical space our mate used to have all to themselves at least by day.

The positive side of retirement is its gift of time, the time to do all those things our work responsibilities have for years prevented us from doing. There is time also to be together in a more leisurely manner, both to play and to continue to make our contributions to the human community.

Retirement calls for yet another new marriage contract, for a fresh division of responsibilities, for agreements about a mutually acceptable balance of togetherness and separateness, for decisions about new undertakings both individual and joint. It calls for a lot of patience with one another as we struggle to adapt to all this change.

By the time we retire, most of us are getting up in years. And so the challenges and opportunities we face at this stage converge with those of aging together, to which we now turn.

EXERCISE 19: THE LIFE LINE

Draw a life line or life inventory and share the results with one another. This is a good way to access hopes, plans, dreams, regrets, and other aspects of life couples seldom talk about. You will need at least two hours of uninterrupted time to do this exercise. Set aside an hour for completing your individual life inventories, and an hour for sharing. If you cannot find one block of time for them, the two parts can be done on separate occasions.

These guidelines from Richard Nelson Bolles' *The Three Boxes of Life* (Berkeley: Ten Speed Press, 1981) may help your reflections. Below is a line, divided into time-segments, which you are asked to consider as representing your life.

Birth 5 10 15 20 25 30 35 40 45 50 55 60 65 70 75 80 85 90 95

1. What moments on the life line stand out in sharpest detail in your memory?
2. What faces from your past can you see most clearly? Whose voices can you hear most vividly? Which of these did you trust the most? Whom did you want to be most like?
3. Which were the events which moved you most

deeply? Which were the events which molded or affected you the most?

4. What were the scenes of your greatest sadnesses? What were the scenes of your deepest joys?

5. What helped to preserve constancy in your life? What helped to promote change?

6. What decision that you made do you feel happiest about? What decision that you made do you regret the most?

Chapter 20

Aging Together

———————— ◇ ————————

Perhaps you nearly decided to skip this chapter because you are not yet old or because you don't like to *think* of yourself as old, whatever your age. When we are really honest with ourselves, most of us admit that we have some fears about aging. But a denial of the aging process merely prevents us from facing some of the challenges and gifts that are part of the last stages of life.

The fact is, we are all aging. During the past century we have added several decades to the human life span. Life expectancy no longer hovers around 46 years, as it did in 1900. By the year 2000, life expectancy in the western nations may be 85. Clearly this creates a very different experience of marriage. Couples can now expect to be together for several decades after their parenting years are completed. Second marriages in late life will become increasingly common.

Since this increased longevity is new to us, there are few ready models to turn to for help in understanding late-life marriage. Moreover, much of what we think about marriage in the later years is influenced by the ageism of our churches and society, an attitude which devalues and discriminates on the basis of age. Yet many older couples are creating their own patterns. We can all learn from their suggestions for enhancing this stage of marriage.

1. *Expect some strains as both of you move through transitions.* A number of transitions cause shifts in our marriage relationship as we age. One of these is the retirement of one or both partners. Another is assuming the role of grandparents. We may also have new physical challenges—loss of hearing or eyesight, or a chronic condition such as arthritis or heart disease. In the later stages of aging, our physical and psychosocial capacities may diminish. In light of increasing physical frailty, we may need to accept an appropriate dependence without losing our trust and hope. These transitions provide new ways for couples to be grace for one another, to be sacraments of God's comfort and challenge in circumstances we might not have foreseen when we first made our promises to one another.

The changes that accompany aging can also place new strains on a relationship. We may resent the restrictions that a partner's physical frailty puts on our freedom or the demands of caregiving it exacts from us. Preoccupation with children and jobs may have allowed us to ignore difficulties in our relationship that we now must face with no buffers. New tensions can revive old quarrels and problems in the relationship that have lingered but never been faced. Retirement may displace normal patterns of responsibility and leave both partners uncomfortable with the new arrangements.

Living through these shifts can call us to a new level of fidelity. It may mean working again on communication, forgiveness, and acceptance. One couple told us that they were in their seventies when they realized that the initial stages of their marriage had never provided an opportunity to establish the kind of intimacy they had hoped for when they married. Children arrived immediately, and the husband had to work several jobs to cover their financial needs. Fatigue and the pressures of parenting interfered with good communication. Now they recognized a longing for that intimacy and began to take the time to nourish it.

2. *Give thanks for the gifts of a lifetime.* This can be a time of thanksgiving and satisfaction in a relationship. We can rejoice in our achievements: pride in having raised children through thick and thin, and joy in grandchildren and great-grandchildren; the sense of self-worth that comes from having surmounted obstacles and setbacks; recognition of the contributions made through one's job and civic involvements; awareness of the twists and turns the relationship has survived. Some couples sum this up succinctly: "We've lived a good life." Others speak of old age as a time of gratitude for the harvest of a long life.

In the seasons of marriage, it is good to experience fully the fruits of this last stage. Couples sometimes enjoy reviewing their lives together, recalling with thanksgiving the gifts they have received, and forgiving themselves and others for their failures.

3. *Find fresh sources of meaning you can share.* Retirement can be a painful transition; it can also open up new opportunities. We once gave a retreat to a group that included a couple in their seventies who were preparing to leave for the Peace Corps. They had decided, now that their children had long been on their own, to capture a dream both had postponed. They wanted to be of service, and decided they would use his engineering skills and her nursing background in another country. Another couple we know established a goal after their retirement of ex-

ploring one new area of knowledge together each year. Right now they are visiting local museums as part of a project to learn more about area artists. This affords them new topics of interest in their relationship, and has also been an avenue to new friendships. Exercising both mind and body stimulates and refreshes them. If we can maintain reasonably good health, the years of aging can be full of creative activity, new work identities, and time to undertake projects made impossible earlier by the demands of our jobs.

For many couples work and family are the central focus throughout earlier years of marriage. Recreation and leisure are at first a welcome relief after years of responsibility. They are not always enough, however, and many of us find that as we age we want to continue to feel that our life has a purpose and meaning beyond ourselves. We ask: "Is this all there is to life?"

The developmental psychologists Erik and Joan Erikson address this concern in their book on *Vital Involvement in Old Age*. Both are in their ninth decades as they write the book, and from that vantage point they ask anew the question of the purpose of our last decades of life. They suggest some of the following potential areas of influence. We can be the bearers of tradition, fostering a sense of continuity among several generations by our stories of the past. Older people, they say, are natural conservationists. The effort to save the natural world needs those with longer memories who can recall the beauty of their surroundings in earlier years. Having seen over time the effects of devastation and aggression, we can be witnesses to the fact that violence is no longer a viable solution for human conflict. These are only some of the common concerns that can bring new energy to marriage.

4. *Continue to enjoy your sexual relationship.* It has always been puzzling why we hold up youthful sexuality and sexual relationships as the ideal in our society. Ageism leads us to fear the signs of aging, the wrinkles and creases in our bodies, and to make the youthful, vigorous body the norm in our images of love. Yet we all know that it takes time to come to a knowledge of our own and our partner's sexuality, and to develop the deeper and subtler dimensions of sexual loving. Likewise, it is one of the gifts of longterm relationships to have sex integrated with years of faithful caring in both good and hard times.

In her works on love and sex in the later years, Barbara Gallatin Anderson asks us to consider that Americans now face decades when our relations with one another as women and men no longer pivot around the parental roles that have been central for many. Those who, like psychiatrist Robert Butler, write about sex in the later years share some common convictions. One is that sex is an important concern in late life, in spite of societal prejudices that portray older persons as uninterested in sex or as physically unattractive and therefore sexually undesirable. Sex becomes not less, but more, important to many older people because they have suffered so many losses. Changes that occur with aging are often misinterpreted, and most sexual difficulties that actually develop are psychological, not physical. It is important to find physicians who are comfortable with conversation around our sexual interest and alert to changes that may affect sexual capacity or to the influence of such factors as side effects from medications.

These changes are usually offset by the lovemaking experience that has been gained over a lifetime, and by the capacity for integrating sex into a relationship. Rob-

ert Butler and Myrna Lewis, in *Love and Sex After Sixty*,
refer to an increased capacity for the second language of
sex. This is sexual expression which is emotional and
communicative as well as physical. It is marked by fuller
knowledge and acceptance of our spouse, and by a deeper
process of communication and caring.

5. Communicate about key ethical choices. As we face
the fact of our aging, we are free to prepare for death and
the dying process, taking those steps now that will assure
us as much dignity and comfort as possible. We face
many challenges together as couples, and during the later
years of our marriage we face our own and our spouse's
mortality. The first elements of this may come as we
notice changes in our physical abilities. One woman recounted to us a conversation she and her husband had
when he experienced some difficulty walking and had to
rely on her for more help. He was bothered by the increased dependence, and said so. Her reply was this: "We
will both be needing one another in new ways as we age.
Let's approach it openly, and not be ashamed to depend
on one another. I like to think of us as in this together."

Some people find it hard to talk about death. But
coming to terms with it helps us know what we want to
do with the rest of our lives. It can also mean a deepening
commitment to the details of love, a realization that we
must say and do now what we might once have put off.
Clear communication about the kind of care we want in
our last stages of life also is the best way to protect our
autonomy and dignity in the dying process. It not only
protects our spouse from the confusion and uncertainty
that come from not knowing what we want, it also allows us to maintain some control over our dying process.
That is why conversation about living wills, power of

attorney, and funeral arrangements are not evidence that we are morbid, but acts of care for ourselves, our spouse, and others who will be affected.

6. *Avoid impossible promises to one another.* As couples face possible illness and lifestyle changes, they sometimes promise one another certain kinds of care. The most common of these promises is a vow that they will never put one another in a nursing home. One partner may extract this from the other, as proof of the partner's love. The problem with such promises is that they tie a spouse to specifics in an unknown future. We have seen many husbands and wives agonize over decisions in light of such a vow. When they can no longer care for a spouse at home, when such care makes impossible demands on their health and finances and those of their children, they still cannot bring themselves to see that a nursing home or other care setting may be the more loving choice. If they must make such a choice, they then struggle with endless guilt regarding it.

Better to trust the love of a spouse and leave them free to work out the details of that love as they are able. This freedom often releases energy that can be directed toward finding good solutions to practical issues.

EXERCISE 20: PRAYER OF THE GRATEFUL HEART

In *Healing the Eight Stages of Life,* Matthew and Dennis Linn and Sheila Fabricant suggest an exercise for individuals that can also be the basis of couple sharing. Take some moments to do the exercise individually, and then close with some joint conversation and prayer around the meaning of the exercise for each of you.

1. Imagine that you are at a slide show. Watch as only pictures of the happy moments of your life appear on the screen. Breathe in once more the "yes" to your life that was in those moments.

2. As your "yes" to your own life deepens, see if some moments appear on the screen that surprise you—moments which at the time seemed meaningless or which you couldn't accept, but which you now see as gifts because of the good that has come from them. As you continue to breathe in your "yes" to the moments you see on the screen, breathe out any feelings of failure or fear that your life has been meaningless.

3. Thank God for the gift of your entire life and the way that all of it has meaning in the divine vision.

Chapter 21

Making a Second Marriage Work

─────── ◇ ───────

About 50 percent of marriages in the western world end in divorce. Approximately 75 percent of divorced persons remarry. So in speaking of second marriages, we treat a topic of relevance to many people.

It is certainly understandable that most individuals whose first marriage came to an end through death or divorce soon wish to be married again. There is the longing for companionship, the yearning for sexual intimacy, the hunger to be special to someone, the need for moral and even financial support in coping with life's demands. Fathers sometimes seek a mother for their children, mothers a father. The good news is that these yearnings are sometimes satisfied, that a second marriage provides a happy ending to a sad story, that people who made a poor first choice make a better one given a second chance. When it happens, it is experienced as one of God's great gifts.

But the statistics on success in second marriages are scarcely more encouraging than those on first marriages. Some 60 percent of them end in divorce. It might be useful to consider the reasons why, so as to slow the rush into second commitments. The point is not to discourage people from marrying again, but to encourage them to take their time, study the matter carefully, and, if they decide they want to do it, prepare themselves and their children for the problems they are most likely to encounter.

Over and above the baggage all of us carry from our family of origin, parties to a second marriage are carrying baggage from the end of their first marriage. It may be unresolved grief. It may be low self-esteem. It may be heightened vulnerability and fear of abandonment. It may be patterns of independence established in the interval since the marriage ended. If divorced individuals are still in a highly-charged negative relationship with their former spouse, they bring yet another stressor to their new situation.

If there are children, the problem is considerably more complicated. Children require time and attention, and the new couple are already taxed with the usual challenges of establishing their own marital relationship. But children in a second marriage require more than ordinary time and attention because they are going through sizable adjustment difficulties of their own. Because these figure so heavily into the life of the new family, it might be useful to detail them before making suggestions on how to make a second marriage work.

The Adjustments the Children Face

There is the divorce itself, which broke up the original family. Long after that event, children often still have fantasies and hopes of their original parents reuniting. Even very young children often carry the additional feeling that they are somehow to blame for the divorce.

If there was a period after the divorce in which children had the custodial parent all to themselves, they naturally resent the intrusion of the new partner who, in a significant way, has taken their parent away from them. Now there is a marriage and that person is living in and probably also exercising authority over them. They had no choice about any of this.

There is the question of belonging. Which home and family do I really belong to? Who are really my parents? Who loves me? Whom do I love? Which rules and expectations am I supposed to follow? If there is conflict between the two households, the situation is still more difficult. Then the children are caught between conflicting loyalties. Love for one parent feels like disloyalty to the other, and may be treated as such by the parents themselves.

There is a loyalty issue also in the home of the custodial parent. The child feels a pressure to love the parent's new mate, and that may be difficult. But not loving that person feels like disloyalty to one's parent.

If both original parents remarry around the same time, the child faces multiple social adjustments all at once. There enter new grandparents, new aunts and uncles, new cousins, new friends. All these people may be well-meaning and affectionate, but it is a lot to adapt to.

There are often new siblings to live with. This touches very close, as these people are right at the table, around the house, possibly even sharing your room. And they may be having their own problems. Perhaps you were the oldest child in your original family, and now are just a middle child. Perhaps you were receiving the attention of the youngest child in your original family, and now there are one or two younger than you. Perhaps you are older, and have just acquired some siblings to take care of. These things are hard to take.

If the children are into puberty, a difficult age as it is, there are additional dilemmas. There may be sexual feelings for a new sibling or for the new step-parent—or the uncomfortable feeling that one of those people has sexual feelings for you. You may have difficulty accepting the more overt sexuality of your original parents, displayed in the relationships they are developing. If you are like most teenagers, you find yourself becoming less interested in your family, more interested in peer relationships. But your moves to pull away from the family collide with your parents' need to build cohesion in the new unit.

With all these stress factors present, it is not surprising that children sometimes regress in second marriages, act out, and consciously or unconsciously find ways to get the attention they need. As they do this, they put added pressure on the family system, particularly on the new couple. This proceeds from their needs and their frustrations, not from their "badness." Nevertheless, their power to divide and even to destroy should not be underestimated.

Making It All Work

The picture just portrayed may seem too bleak to some, worse than the reality could possibly be. We hope it is. In most cases, not all these problems will be present, which makes it easier. But we think it is better to go in with a clear sense of all the problems that may be present and find a few missing, than to anticipate being "one big happy family" only to walk into a hurricane. There follow some suggestions for making a success of it.

1. Keep expectations reasonable. Therapists experienced in working with second marriages seem to agree that there are two main keys to making a second marriage and family work: reasonable expectations and open communication. As Erna Paris stresses in her book, *Stepfamilies*, the principal unreasonable expectation is precisely that we will be one big happy family. But the family that results from a second marriage is not a family in the usual sense. It does not evolve as a first family evolves. It is created by blending already existing elements drawn from previous configurations. And so it has a different internal feeling, and it operates by different rules.

If the persons brought together in a second marriage do succeed in becoming a happy family, it will probably come about only through struggle, and therefore it will not come about quickly. Parents do themselves and their children a great favor when they allow plenty of slack for the necessary adjustments to take place, not expecting comfortable patterns to develop for at least two years. There are problems of space, problems of time, problems of belonging, problems of authority. Even intact families struggle with these issues, often for years. They are still more difficult for blended families.

2. Make open communication a very high priority. This is the second key to success. The new grouping has to make allowance for all feelings and positively invite their expression, fully expecting confusion, pain, ambiguity, and negativity. The more information there is out in the open, the better chance everyone has to understand one another and to work on solutions. It is not helpful to try to talk people out of their feelings, or to present the other side of the matter, until the feelings have at least been heard and validated. Besides feelings and problems that are being experienced, another helpful component of these conversations is the exchange of personal histories. Since each of us is the product of our history, sharing our story really helps others understand and get some feeling for us. Very young children can be helped in this sharing by their parent.

3. Make use of professional counseling. Counseling can be a tremendous help in this enterprise of forming good working bonds among members of the new family, and it should begin before the developing family take up living together. Starting with the new couple, then incorporating the children, an experienced facilitator can establish an atmosphere in which everyone can begin to talk about what really concerns them and share their true feelings. It is a setting in which everyone will be encouraged to name the difficulties they are already experiencing and the hopes and fears they bring to the new situation. Facilitation helps especially when painful feelings are expressed and people feel attacked or threatened, or when feelings are for some reason not being heard and need amplification and validation. An experienced counselor can normalize what would otherwise feel alarming, and help a family toward both reasonable expectations and practical solutions. It also helps to do some reading on the subject, and we offer a few suggestions at the end of the book.

4. A stepparent should be slow to move into an authority role. A stepparent is wise not to expect quick acceptance, let alone affection, and to work quite a while at bonding with the children as a friend before moving into any kind of authority role. Where a child is acting out or showing special needs, the natural parent should be in charge, the stepparent working in a supportive capacity.

A rule of thumb which has developed among those experienced in working with blended families is that a child needs as many years as he or she is old to come to relate to the new parent as a real parent—a three-year old three years, a ten-year old ten. It is because they have already had that much life-experience that you were no part of. The first victory you need to win is their acceptance of you as a person; the second, their acceptance of you as an authority figure. It is most unwise to enter the lives of someone else's children intending either to "restore order" or to be "the parent they never had." The reality is, you are entering the lives of children painfully suffering a broken situation. You may give a great deal of love and service before you see much of anything coming back. And even when acceptance shall be complete and love runs deep, you are still not, nor ever will be, their natural parent.

5. *Make peace with your ex-spouse.* Any reduction of hostility and mistrust here pays a huge emotional dividend to the two of you, your children, and all others concerned. The point was brought home to us recently when a couple came in for therapy some three or four years after their divorce. They sought a better reconciliation with each other and healing for themselves from all the pain of their divorce. They felt called upon to do this as Christians, as parents of the children they were still raising together, and as two individuals who wanted to bring more personal wholeness to new relationships.

To accomplish their goal, they had to go back and process the pain each felt in the deterioration and ultimate ending of their marriage, reviewing the history and naming the disappointments and hurt each had sustained at the other's hands. Hard as that was to listen to nondefensively, it gave both of them a much clearer understanding of how their love had broken down and what each of them had to work on to make a new relationship work better. When each took responsibility and apologized for the ways they had failed the other, they found they could forgive each other, and, with this formerly unresolved pain now drained away, could cooperate as parents on a much more congenial basis.

6. *Keep making time to nurture your own relationship.* Therapists Emily and John Visher, in their book, *Stepfamilies*, lay great stress on the importance of a strong couple bond to make a blended family work. It may seem an impossible additional demand to ask that you keep making time to nurture your own relationship, but success here is the foundation of everything else. It was with each other that you first fell in love, and it is a strong emotional bond and teamwork that you most need to hold the whole family together. Precisely because the challenges you face are so great, and the occasions for being pulled apart by conflicting loyalties and differing philosophies so multiple, you need to keep nurturing the bond. You may need some time apart just to strategize and solve problems. But don't let all your time together get burned up that way. You need some fun.

EXERCISE 21: DAILY DIALOGUE

David and Vera Mace, who have worked in marital therapy for decades, report that in their own marriage they instituted a daily exercise which has helped them stay emotionally attuned to one another and keep misunderstandings to a minimum. They spend twenty minutes a day, ten and ten, just sharing *all* the feelings that have been coursing through their awareness. Each just listens to the other.

They do not use this as a forum for dealing with strong anger or difficult issues; that they do separately. They do mention small "twinges" or "pinches" that have occurred in their interaction just for the other's information. But they see this daily exercise as an exchange with a very broad purpose, that of simply keeping each other informed of what is going on inside day to day, so that each knows what is happening and can be attuned to the other. It prevents surprises and blowups, and fosters intimacy.

Chapter 22

Finding the Fun in It All

◇

Joyce Hollyday, an editor of *Sojourners* magazine and a member of the Sojourners Community in inner-city Washington, D.C., tells a story that comes from a Salvadoran refugee camp in Honduras. A friend of hers from the United States had been working in the camp for several months when one of the refugee women asked her why she always looked so sad and burdened. The woman replied by recounting all the suffering she had seen, detailing her despair at trying to keep her commitment to the struggle of the refugees.

The refugee woman then gently chided her: "Only people who expect to go back to North America in a year work the way you do. You cannot be serious about our struggle unless you play and celebrate and do those things that make it possible to give a lifetime to it." The woman reminded the worker that each time refugees were displaced and had to build a new camp, they formed three committees: a construction committee, an education committee, and the *comité de alegria*—the "committee of joy." Celebration was as basic to their life as digging the latrines and teaching their children to read.

Part of the common wisdom often handed down to couples is that you have to work at marriage. A good marriage doesn't just happen. This is true. Marriage calls for many things which require effort. But what this Honduran story teaches us about peace and justice work is also true for marriage. If we are to be faithful over time, we must make room for joy and celebration.

In marriage, as in life, there must be times of rest and play. A walk along a lake, a game of volleyball, sharing a meal out—these all nourish a marriage relationship as much as developing communication skills and learning to resolve differences. Married intimacy is deepened by moments of shared wonder at the beauty of a winter sunset or the first spring buds on bushes and trees, by times of mutual excitement over a piece of music or a painting. In fact, when things aren't going well, it may be a sign that we need to lighten up and have more fun together. Here are a few ideas to help you find the fun in your marriage.

1. New Interests, New Activities

Over the long haul, every marriage needs occasional injections of fresh interests and activities the couple share. It may feel a little strange and even uninviting to one of you at first, but you can learn to enjoy new things. Some couples join athletic clubs and exercise together. Some run together. Some sign up for cooking classes. Some take dancing.

After Tom's dad retired, his parents began teaching bridge to elderly groups. Also, in their last years, they spent one day a week visiting their elderly friends in nursing homes. We ourselves expanded a longstanding interest in classical music to a deep love of opera, and now have season tickets and own numerous operas as well.

Some couples begin Bible study with a group. Others volunteer for parish leadership positions. Some get interested in the neighborhood soup kitchen, or in tutoring underprivileged children. Some read and discuss books together, by themselves or with another couple or two. Some take up hiking, or city walks. Some travel. There are any number of possibilities. Somebody just needs to think creatively and nudge the inertia.

2. Marriage Enrichment

Make a retreat together, or each make one separately. Quiet time away makes you think, and new infusions of spiritual life always seem to pick up a marriage even if marriage is not their primary focus. Make a marriage enrichment event, whether it be Marriage Encounter or some other form of renewal. Read a book on marriage every year and discuss it. Read a book on sexual relating, discuss your own sexuality in light of it, and try some of the exercises the book suggests. Form a small group of married couples who trust one another and know how to keep confidences, and get together every month or two to talk about marital issues.

3. Special Times

These are celebrations of birthdays and anniversaries, evenings out, weekends away without the children. Managing such events when money is limited often requires creativity. Yet couples who know the importance of it manage it. They find that fun does not have to cost very much, and the simplest of activities—a gift of flowers, flying kites, visiting the zoo or a museum—can renew their spirits and rekindle the energy between them.

4. Humor and Play

The child within each of us needs to play. Sex is part of that play. So are baseball games, card games, movies. What frees up the child in your relationship, and shows you the crazy and delightful sides of each other? Nobody can escape the work component of marriage. It would be a shame if the play component got crowded out.

Our own marriage is characterized by a lot of word play. If you were alone with us, you would hear expressions like: "How did you ever make it in the world before you met me?" "Do you like me today?" "Gimme that, you fool!" "I know I'd be happier with a younger man." These are not things said in anger. They are said in fun, and they make us smile. They are deliberately outrageous. They salt the banal exchanges of daily life, and keep us in contact when there is nothing important to say. Many couples have a private, playful language of this kind.

It is also important to be able to find the humor in the many events that frustrate and irritate us. One woman, who has been married for over fifty years, found a technique for bringing laughter into her marriage relationship. She made it a practice to cut out cartoons that portrayed the various dilemmas they faced, and she often put one next to her husband's coffee cup in the morning. "We learned," she said, "that it doesn't pay to take ourselves too seriously. Marriage cannot survive without the kind of perspective that humor brings. The cartoons helped us see ourselves with both compassion and realism. Most of all, they provided the tonic of hearty, shared laughter." Laughter is indeed a tonic. It is an essential element in physical and emotional health, and it is an important aspect of good communication.

Humor allows us to recognize that limitations and failures are not final and unredeemable tragedies. It is a gentle reminder of the reality of redemption. Humor also opens us to the sacred, and suggests God's abiding presence in our marriage. Since it both acknowledges our finiteness and at the same time transcends it, humor reveals that there is a *more* in the midst of human life. It points, in other words, to something we have called attention to repeatedly in this book. It is God's grace, finally: that is the ground of our lives in marriage.

EXERCISE 22: THE SURPRISE LIST

One of the things that brings fun and laughter into our lives is surprises. In *Getting the Love You Want*, Harville Hendrix gives these directions for developing a surprise list for your mate.

1. Make a list of things you could do for your partner that would be fun and pleasing. Don't guess. Draw up your list from your memory of things that have pleased your partner in the past or from hints or comments your partner has made. Become a detective and ferret out your partner's concealed wishes and desires. Keep your list hidden from your partner at all times.

2. Select one item and surprise your partner with it this week. Be sure to do this at least once a week and at random times, so that your partner will have difficulty anticipating the surprise.

3. Record the date when you gave each surprise.

4. On a separate sheet of paper, record and date the surprises you receive from your partner. Thank your partner each time they surprise you.

Suggestions for Further Reading

Lonnie Barbach, *For Each Other: Sharing Sexual Intimacy* (Anchor, 1982).

Rosemary Curran Barciauskas and Debra Hull, *Loving and Working* (Meyer Stone, 1989).

Harold Bloomfield and Sirah Vetesse, *Lifemates* (New American, 1989).

Robert Butler and Myrna Lewis, *Love and Sex After Sixty* (Harper, 1976).

Susan Campbell, *The Couples' Journey* (Impact, 1980).

Katherine Dyckman and Patrick Carroll, *Chaos or Creation: Spirituality in Mid-Life* (Paulist, 1986).

Albert Ellis, *Anger* (Citadel, 1977).

Kathleen Fischer and Thomas Hart, *The First Two Years of Marriage* (Paulist, 1983).

Harville Hendrix, *Getting the Love You Want* (Henry Holt, 1988).

Mel Krantzler, *Creative Marriage* (McGraw Hill, 1981).

Arnold Lazarus, *Marital Myths* (Impact, 1985).

Madeleine L'Engle, *Two-Part Invention: The Story of a Marriage* (Farrar, 1988).

Harriet Lerner, *The Dance of Anger* (Perennial, 1986).

Harriet Lerner, *The Dance of Intimacy* (Harper, 1989).

Dennis and Matthew Linn and Sheila Fabricant Linn, *Healing the Eight Stages of Life* (Paulist, 1988).

David Mace, *Love and Anger in Marriage* (Zondervan, 1982).

W. Hugh Missildine, *Your Inner Child of the Past* (Pocket Books, 1963).

Gene and Judith Tate O'Brien, *Couples Praying* (Paulist, 1986).

Anthony Padovano, *Love and Destiny* (Paulist, 1987).

Erna Paris, *Stepfamilies* (Avon, 1984).
John Powell, *The Secret of Staying in Love* (Argus, 1974).
Challon O'Hearn and William P. Roberts, *Partners in Intimacy* (Paulist, 1988).
Lillian Rubin, *Intimate Strangers* (Perennial, 1983).
Emily and John Visher, *Stepfamilies* (Citadel, 1979).
Evelyn Eaton and James D. Whitehead, *Marrying Well* (Doubleday, 1981).
Evelyn Eaton and James D. Whitehead, *A Sense of Sexuality* (Doubleday, 1989).
Bernie Zilbergeld, *Male Sexuality* (Bantam, 1978).